THE USBORNE
ENCYCLOPEDIA OF
ANCIENT
GREECE

The remains of the Temple of
Apollo at Delphi, Greece, built in
the 4th century BC

THE USBORNE ENCYCLOPEDIA OF ANCIENT GREECE

Jane Chisholm, Lisa Miles and Struan Reid

Designed by Linda Penny, Laura Fearn
and Melissa Alaverdy

Illustrated by Inklink Firenze, Ian Jackson, Giacinto Gaudenzi,
Jeremy Gower, Nick Harris, Nicholas Hewetson and Rodney Matthews

Consultant: Dr. Anne Millard

Managing designer: Stephen Wright

Cover design: Hannah Ahmed and Zöe Wray

Digital images: John Russell   Picture research: Ruth King

With thanks to Anna Claybourne and Abigail Wheatley

CONTENTS

INTERNET LINKS

Throughout this book we have suggested interesting websites where you can find out more about the ancient Greeks. You'll find descriptions of the recommended websites in the Internet Links boxes on the pages of this book, and there are links to all the websites at the **Usborne Quicklinks Website.**

USBORNE QUICKLINKS

To visit the websites, follow these simple instructions to go to the **Usborne Quicklinks Website.**

1. Go to **www.usborne-quicklinks.com**
2. Type the keywords for this book: **ancient greece**
3. Type the page number of the links you want to visit.
4. Click on the links to go to the websites.

Here are some of the things you can do on the websites recommended in this book:

- Explore ancient Athens with an interactive map and discover what it was like to live there.

- Learn how to speak like an ancient Greek and translate Greek names in an online game.

- Build a temple online, design a Greek pot, command a Greek trireme or try other fascinating online activities.

- Take a virtual trip to the ancient Olympic Games.

- Try online games and quizzes about Greek gods and goddesses, and find out more about them

- Follow an animated story of Odysseus' travels.

INTERNET SAFETY

Ask your parent's or guardian's permission before you connect to the Internet and make sure you follow these simple rules:

- Never give out information about yourself, such as your real name, address, phone number or the name of your school.

- If a site asks you to log in or register by typing your name or email address, ask permission from an adult first.

Please read and follow the Internet safety guidelines on the Usborne Quicklinks Website.

NOTE FOR PARENTS

The websites described in this book are regularly reviewed, but the content of a website may change at any time and Usborne Publishing is not responsible for the content on any website other than its own.

We recommend that children are supervised while on the Internet, that they do not use Internet chat rooms, and that you use Internet filtering software to block unsuitable material. Please ensure that your children read and follow the safety guidelines printed above. For more information, see the Net Help area on the Usborne Quicklinks Website.

RealPlayer® is a registered trademark of RealNetworks, Inc.
Windows Media® player is a registered trademark of Microsoft Corporation in the United States and/or other countries.
Adobe®Flash® is the registered trademark of Adobe Systems Incorporated in the United States and/or other countries.

SITE AVAILABILITY

The links in Usborne Quicklinks are regularly reviewed and updated, but occasionally you may get a message that a site is unavailable. This might be temporary, so try again later. If a website closes down, we will replace it with a new link. Sometimes we add extra links too, so when you visit Usborne Quicklinks, the links may be slightly different from those described in your book.

WHAT YOU NEED

To visit the websites you need a computer with an Internet connection and a web browser (the software that lets you look at information on the Internet).

To view video clips and animations and listen to sounds, you may need small, free programs called 'plug-ins'. For example, to watch video clips and listen to sounds, you need Windows Media® player or RealPlayer®. For playing animations you need a plug-in called 'Flash'.

If you go to a website and do not have the necessary plug-in, a message will come up on the screen. There is usually a link to click on to download the plug-in.

For more information about plug-ins, go to the Usborne Quicklinks Website and click on 'Net Help'.

INTERNET HELP

For help using the Internet and Usborne Quicklinks, go to the Net Help area on the Usborne Quicklinks Website. There you will find links and information on how to keep your computer up to date, and tips on how to browse the Internet safely and securely.

You will also find links to download the free 'plug-in' programs you may need to play sounds or video clips (see left). There are step-by-step instructions for installing and setting up the plug-ins, and advice on downloading pictures from the Internet and using them in your schoolwork.

For more help on using your web browser and the Internet, click on 'Help' in the menu at the top of your web browser. There you will find a huge, searchable database of information.

COMPUTER VIRUSES

A computer virus is a small program that can seriously damage your computer. A virus can get into your computer when you download programs from the Internet, or in an attachment that arrives with an email.

We strongly recommend that you buy anti-virus software to protect your computer, and that you update the anti-virus software regularly to guard your computer against new viruses.

To find out more about viruses, go to the Net Help area on the Usborne Quicklinks Website.

HOW WE KNOW ABOUT THE GREEKS

The civilization with the greatest influence on the development of the modern world was probably ancient Greece. Although it came to an end more than 2,000 years ago, historians still know a great deal about the ancient Greeks and their lives.

This archaeologist is carefully brushing the dirt from pots and skeletons found in this Greek tomb.

BURIED SECRETS

Ancient Greek towns and cities have been dug up all over Greece and in Greek colonies like southern Italy. Archaeologists have unearthed the remains of thousands of objects and buildings - both on land and at sea.

Marine archaeologists have explored the wrecks of several Greek ships, with their cargoes amazingly preserved.

This marine archaeologist is exploring a shipwreck in the Aegean Sea.

Greek objects have also been found in countries where they were taken by traders. For instance, pots made on Crete have turned up in Egyptian tombs.

PICTURE POTS

The Greeks were famous for their pottery, which they decorated with scenes from mythology and everyday life. These have provided vast amounts of information about their lives, the clothes they wore, their houses and furniture.

Greek pot, called an amphora, showing mythological creatures

Archaeologists use aerial shots - like this one of Olympia, site of the first Olympic Games - to make drawings, models and computer-generated reconstructions.

ROMAN COPIES

When the Romans occupied Greece in the 2nd century BC, they were so impressed by Greek art and architecture that they made thousands of copies of what they found. Although many Greek originals have been lost, a large number of Roman copies have survived.

WRITTEN EVIDENCE

The Greeks were prolific writers - on history, politics, philosophy and literature - but few of their manuscripts have survived. So again historians rely on the Romans, who made copies of Greek writings, on coins, clay tablets and public monuments.

Greek coin showing a charioteer

MAP OF ANCIENT GREECE

ILLYRIA

THRACE

MACEDONIA

Methone

Vergina

Pydna

CHALCIDICE

Hellespont

Aegospotami

Granicus

Troy

Mount
Olympus

EPIRUS

Dodona

THESSALY

Iolkos

AEGEAN SEA

LESBOS

Pergamum

CORCYRA

EUBOEA

SKYROS

Smyrna

Thermopylae

ITHACA

Delphi

Thebes

Eretria

CHIOS

IONIA

Chaeronea

Plataea

Marathon

Leuctra

ACHAEA

Corinth

Athens

ATTICA

SAMOS

Ephesus

Elis

Mycenae

Salamis

Aegina

Mantinea

Argos

Epidaurus

Miletus

Olympia

ARCADIA

Tiryns

ARGOLIS

DELOS

Halicarnassus

MESSENIA

CYCLADIC ISLANDS

Sparta

KOS

NAXOS

Pylos

Cnidus

LACONIA

MEDITERRANEAN SEA

THERA

CRETE

Knossos

Mallia

Zakro

Hagia Triada

Phaestos

EARLY GREECE

THE FIRST GREEKS

Greece is a hot, dry, country in southern Europe with a craggy, mountainous landscape. Its long, jagged coastline, peppered with bays and inlets, juts out into the Mediterranean Sea and is surrounded by hundreds of islands. Around 40,000 years ago, the first inhabitants started moving into the area.

THE STONE AGE

The first Greeks lived in caves and used tools of bone and flint. They hunted bison and reindeer - which have long since died out in southern Europe - and gathered wild plants. This period is known as the Stone Age.

THE FIRST FARMERS

Some time before 6000BC, farmers settled in eastern Greece. They grew wheat and vegetables, and kept sheep. The landscape wasn't quite the same as it is now: it was much more wooded, and the only good farming land was in narrow valleys and coastal plains. So people relied on fishing for extra food.

THE BRONZE AGE

Around 3000BC, people in Greece discovered how to make bronze by mixing copper and tin. They used it to make tools and weapons that were hard and sharp. This made farming and building easier. This period, from around 3000BC to 1100BC, is known as the Bronze Age.

A Bronze Age gold earring

THE FIRST TOWNS

As farming became more efficient, many farmers grew more food than their families could eat. This extra food could be exchanged for other goods, such as tools or pottery. Some people began to make a living as craftsmen, making objects instead of farming. The population increased and some villages grew into towns.

Fish-hook

Scraper

Dagger

A selection of bone tools

INTERNET LINKS

For links to websites where you can see carved figures from the Cyclades, as well as pots shaped like animals, go to **www.usborne-quicklinks.com**

This map shows the Greek mainland and islands.

THE CYCLADES

Archaeologists have identified a thriving culture on the Cyclades islands from about 2600-2000BC. Craftsmen there produced fine carvings and there was active trade between the islands. But the Cyclades were too small for the way of life there to develop further.

This stretch of the Greek coastline, looking out onto the Aegean Sea, looks much the same as it did when the first Greeks settled here.

A marble figure from the Cyclades, dating back to about 2500BC

THE MINOANS

The first ever European civilization developed on Crete, the largest of the Greek islands. It began to flourish around the year 2000BC, but mysteriously died out less than a thousand years later. Its remains were first discovered in the 1920s, by a British archaeologist, Sir Arthur Evans. He named it the Minoan civilization, after a legendary king of Crete named Minos.

MINOAN LIFE

Minoan civilization was based around several large palaces, each of which was at the heart of a thriving local community - with skilled craftsmen, artists, and professional writers known as scribes. The Minoans also had a highly organized economy and system of trade. Their goods have been found all over Greece, the Cyclades islands, Egypt and the eastern Mediterranean.

Much of what we know about the Minoan way of life comes from frescoes (wall paintings). It appears that most people made their living from farming, but fished and hunted for extra food. We also know that men usually wore a loincloth and a short kilt made of wool or linen, while women wore bright dresses with frilled skirts.

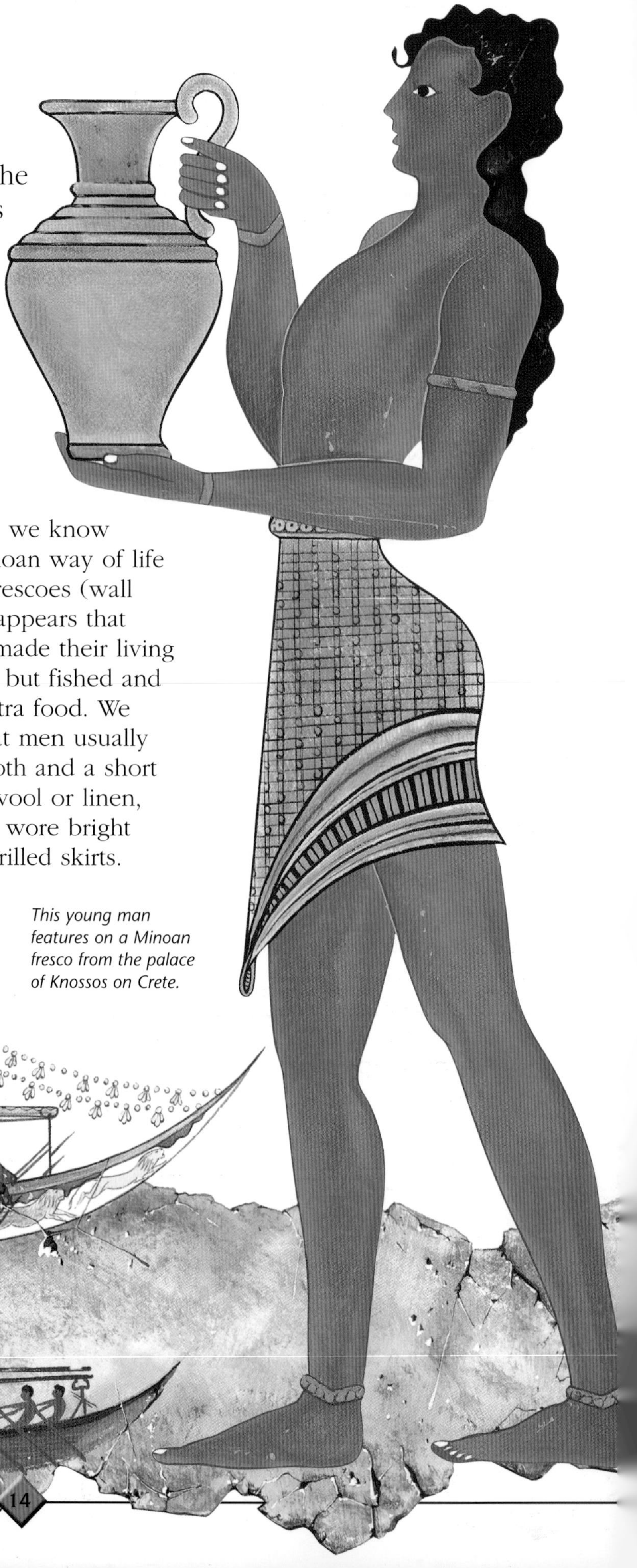

This young man features on a Minoan fresco from the palace of Knossos on Crete.

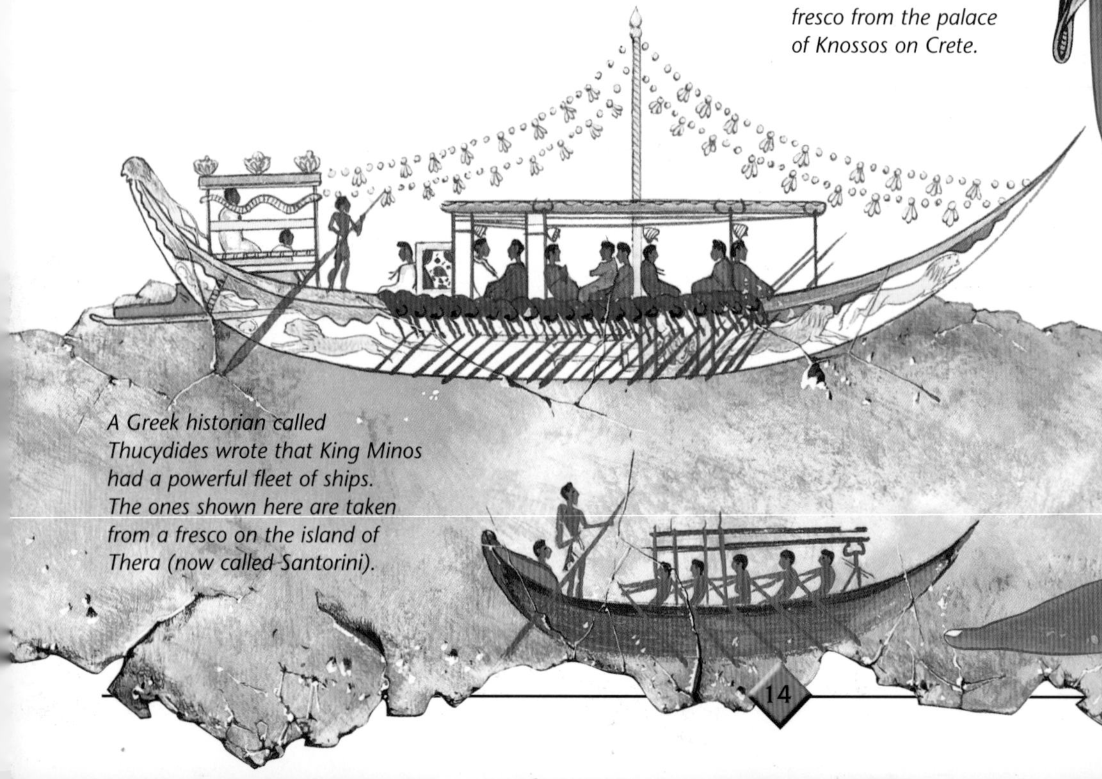

A Greek historian called Thucydides wrote that King Minos had a powerful fleet of ships. The ones shown here are taken from a fresco on the island of Thera (now called Santorini).

THE LEGEND OF MINOS

According to Greek legend, the god Zeus fell in love with a beautiful princess called Europa. Zeus turned himself into the shape of a bull and swam to Crete with her on his back. One of their three sons, Minos, became the King of Crete. Although Minos was the name of the king in the legend, scholars think *Minos* may have been a Cretan title for all kings, like the Egyptian word *Pharaoh*.

Europa riding on the back of Zeus

 INTERNET LINKS

For links to websites where you can see Minoan pottery, paintings and jewels, and explore an interactive map about trade, go to www.usborne-quicklinks.com

MINOAN HOUSES

At the heart of Minoan life was the palace, where the royal family lived. Courtiers and people who worked at the palace also lived there, but most people would have lived in houses outside the palace grounds. The storage and cooking areas were downstairs, with the living and sleeping areas above.

This model house, found at the palace at Knossos, is made of faience (glazed earthenware). It shows what Minoan town houses probably looked like.

DATING THE EVIDENCE

Archaeologists sometimes use information from other cultures to help them date newly excavated sites. Minoan pots had been found in Egypt, long before any major sites were found on Crete. So, when similar pots were eventually discovered on Crete, experts were able to date them according to the Egyptian finds.

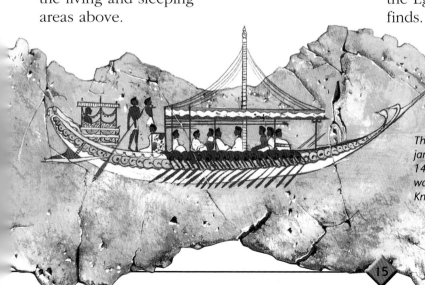

This Minoan jar, dated 1450-1400BC, was dug up in Knossos.

MINOAN PALACES

Around 2000BC, the Minoans built several large palaces, each with its own king and royal family. These remained the focus of their communities and their way of life until around 1700BC, when disaster struck the island and the palaces were destroyed by a series of earthquakes. The Minoans remained undeterred, however, and built new, even grander, palaces right on top of the ruins of the old ones.

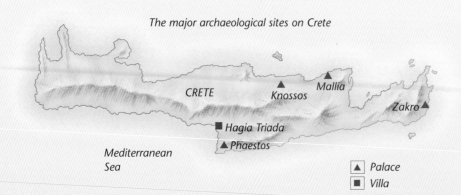

The major archaeological sites on Crete

CRETE
Knossos
Mallia
Zakro
Hagia Triada
Phaestos

Mediterranean Sea

▲ Palace
■ Villa

FRESCOES

Each palace had apartments set aside for its royal family. These were spacious rooms decorated with wall paintings known as frescoes, made by applying paint to wet plaster. The frescoes at Knossos have given archaeologists lots of valuable information about Minoan life. Most of the frescos you can see there today, however, are actually modern reconstructions.

INTERNET LINKS

For a link to a website where you can take a virtual tour of the palace of Knossos, go to **www.usborne-quicklinks.com**

KNOSSOS

The largest of the Minoan palaces was at Knossos, which was built and rebuilt several times. The walls were mainly stone, with wooden roofs, ceilings and doors. The design of the palace was light and airy, with a good drainage system, and it was decorated with bulls' horns – which appear to have been a Minoan religious symbol. At its height, over 30,000 people may have lived in Knossos and surrounding areas.

This fresco shows a young man who was probably a prince or a king.

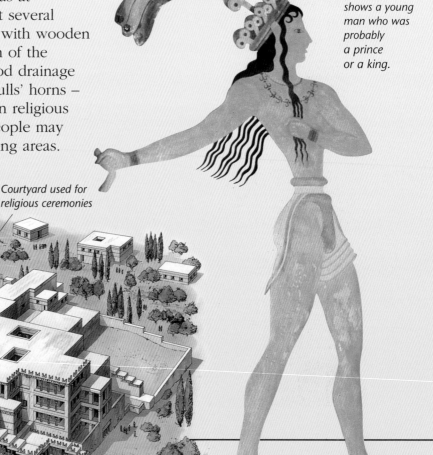

The palace at Knossos

Courtyard used for religious ceremonies

THE KING

The King of Knossos may have had some authority over the rulers of the other palaces, and played an important part in the religious life of the whole island. He had a number of state apartments, including a throne room where state business and religious ceremonies took place.

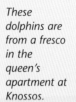

These dolphins are from a fresco in the queen's apartment at Knossos.

THE HARVEST

As a form of tax, the king retained part of the annual grain harvest, which was stored at the palace. A portion of it was used to feed the people who lived there, and to pay officials and craftsmen.

The rest was exported around the Mediterranean, and the profits were used to pay for imports from other countries, such as precious metals, jewels, ostrich feathers, ivory and amber.

A large pot, called a pithos, used for storing food and wine

The throne room at Knossos was discovered almost intact. This is what it looks like today.

MINOAN SCRIPTS

The Minoans developed writing systems to help them keep records for trading purposes. The first, from c.2000BC, was a form of hieroglyphic (picture) writing. From c.1900BC, they began using a script which we call Linear A. So far, however, no one has been able to decipher either of the scripts.

Linear A clay tablet from Hagia Triada, dated c.1900BC

MINOAN RELIGION

This bull's head is actually a vessel, called a rhyton. It was used for pouring liquid offerings to the gods.

Although there are no written records of the Minoans' religious beliefs, we know certain things from their paintings, pots and statues.

Double-headed weapon, called a labrys

SACRED SYMBOLS

There appear to have been two main sacred symbols. One was the bull, sacred to the sea god. Images of its horns were found all over Knossos. The other sacred symbol was a double-headed weapon, known as a *labrys*. Both of these were used to decorate pots and tombs, as well as palaces.

RELIGIOUS CEREMONIES

Religious ceremonies were led by priests and priestesses, while musicians played. Rooms were set aside for worship in the palaces, but Minoans also used outdoor shrines in caves and on mountain tops.

It seems likely that goddesses and priestesses were more important than gods and priests. We know this because females are shown more prominently in religious statues and paintings.

INTERNET LINKS

For a link to a website where you can find out more about Minoan religion and see pictures of Minoan priests, go to **www.usborne-quicklinks.com**

Bulls' horns symbol from the palace of Knossos

This small marble statue is probably a Minoan priestess.

BULL-LEAPING

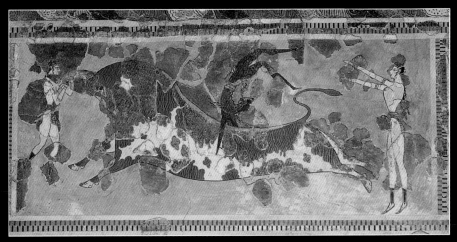

This fresco from Knossos shows a man leaping over a bull's back. The figure on the left held the bull's horns, while the figure on the right caught the leaper.

The Minoans appear to have had a daring custom, which involved leaping over a bull. From images on Minoan paintings, it seems that teams of men and women took turns to approach a charging bull. They grasped its horns and catapulted themselves onto its back, and then onto the ground. This dangerous sport may have been a religious ritual, as the bull was a sacred animal. It probably took place in the courtyard of the palace.

DEATH AND THE AFTERLIFE

The Minoans believed in life after death. They buried their dead with food and possessions, for use in the afterlife. In early times, the rich were buried in stone tombs with other bodies. Later on, they were buried in individual coffins.

This coffin, dated c.1400BC, was found in Hagia Triada on Crete. It is decorated with a funeral scene, showing people making offerings.

THE LEGEND OF THE MINOTAUR

According to legend, an Athenian prince named Theseus sailed to Crete, where he fought and overpowered a terrible monster known as the Minotaur. The monster was half man and half bull and was kept in a labyrinth – an underground maze.

This tale may be based partly on fact. The palace at Knossos was so maze-like that it could be described as a labyrinth. The king may also have worn a bull's mask in religious ceremonies, linking him to the idea of the Minotaur.

EXPLOSIONS AND INVASIONS

Around 1600BC, the once golden age of Minoan culture went into decline. Although we don't know exactly why this happened, it seems that Crete suffered a series of natural disasters which must have contributed.

THERA EXPLODES

Scientists have discovered that, around 1450BC, the nearby island of Thera was blasted to pieces by a massive volcanic eruption. At about the same time, the palaces on Crete were destroyed. The cause may have been tidal waves and earth tremors, created by the eruption - but, whatever the reason, the whole Minoan way of life was thrown into chaos.

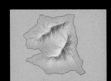

Thera before the eruption

Thera after the eruption

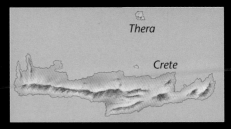

Thera (the main part of which is now called Santorini) is 110km (70 miles) from Crete.

 **INTERNET LINKS**

For a link to a website where you can explore the ruins of Akrotiri on Thera and look at more frescoes and pottery, go to
www.usborne-quicklinks.com

The explosion on Thera may have been the biggest volcanic eruption in 10,000 years. People would have been killed, farmland ruined by falling ash, and houses destroyed.

MYCENAEANS INVADE

After the Thera eruption, the Minoans seem to have reoccupied their palaces for a time - until, around 1350BC, when most of the palaces and villas were destroyed for good, this time by fire. We don't know what caused this, but it is likely that Crete was invaded by Mycenaeans from mainland Greece, who overthrew the Minoans and took control of the island, destroying the Minoan civilization in the process.

Mycenaean pot, discovered on the Greek mainland, showing a military scene

AKROTIRI

In the 1960s, Greek archaeologists Spyridon Marinatos and Christos Doumas started excavations on Thera. They unearthed the remains of a Minoan village at Akrotiri, which had been completely buried in volcanic ash. Houses, frescoes and pottery were all preserved, revealing in great detail how Minoan people lived their lives.

Minoan houses in Akrotiri on the island of Thera

A fresco showing blue monkeys, from a house in Akrotiri

THE END OF KNOSSOS

Knossos became the focus of Mycenaean society on Crete, but around 1100BC it was burned down and never rebuilt. No one knows what caused the fire, but it could have been the result of a violent confrontation between Mycenaeans and Minoans, or between different Mycenaean groups.

THE LEGEND OF ATLANTIS

According to the Greek philosopher Plato, there was a once thriving civilization on an island named Atlantis, which had sunk beneath the ocean without trace. Over the centuries, many people have been captivated by the legend - with some suggesting that the eruption and the departure of the Minoans might be the source of the story.

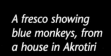

17th century map, based on Plato's story, showing Atlantis in the Atlantic Ocean, between Europe and North America

THE MYCENAEANS

From about 1600BC, mainland Greece was dominated by a people we call the Mycenaeans. They are named after the city of Mycenae, where evidence of their culture was first discovered.

INTERNET LINKS

For a link to a website where you can take a virtual tour of Mycenae, go to **www.usborne-quicklinks.com**

Map of Mycenaean cities

GREECE
Iolkos
Orchomenos
Gla Thebes
Mycenae Athens Miletus
Dendra
Pylos
Sparta
Mediterranean Sea CRETE

THE ACROPOLIS

The acropolis at Mycenae was similar to those of other ancient cities. Inside the walls was the royal palace and houses for courtiers, soliders and craftsmen. The main gateway was decorated with two lions, possibly symbols of the royal family.

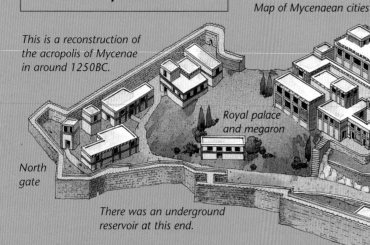

This is a reconstruction of the acropolis of Mycenae in around 1250BC.

City walls, extended in the 13th century BC

Houses

Circular wall enclosing graves

Royal palace and megaron

North gate

There was an underground reservoir at this end.

The Lion Gate

WHO WERE THEY?

The Mycenaeans lived in small kingdoms, each based around a separate city. These kingdoms were never united, but they traded together and shared a language and way of life. Mycenae itself was probably the leading city.

Historians are not sure where the Mycenaeans came from. They may have come to Greece from central Europe around 2000BC, or they may have already been in Greece for some time before that.

WHERE DID THEY LIVE?

Most Mycenaeans lived in walled cities which were built on high ground, to make them easy to defend. The important buildings were situated in the *acropolis* (meaning "high city" in Greek) on top of the hill. Most people lived in the lower town, outside the walls of the acropolis.

FOOD AND TRADE

As in Crete, the palace was at the heart of the island's economic life. Craftsmen's goods and produce from farming were stored in the acropolis, for distribution around Crete, or export.

A gold pot, called a rhyton, shaped like an animal's head

MYCENAEAN PALACE LIFE

This is a reconstruction of a megaron, based on excavations from several cities.

The royal palace at Mycenae was made up of several brightly painted buildings - often with more than one floor - arranged around a vast central courtyard. A Mycenaean palace was far more than just a royal residence. It was a military headquarters, an administrative base, and a workplace for craftsmen. Palace life revolved around a large hall, called a megaron, where the king held court and conducted state business.

This fresco shows a woman courtier, from Mycenae.

MYCENAEAN SCRIPT

The Mycenaeans adapted Minoan forms of writing to devise their own script, which we call Linear B. Archaeologists have unearthed thousands of Linear B tablets, which they have been able to decipher, because the Mycenaeans spoke an early form of Greek.

Linear B clay tablet

The results have not been that exciting, though, as the tablets mainly contain lists - of livestock, farming produce and craft items, as well as details of palace officials and their tasks.

MYCENAEAN ROYAL TOMBS

In 1876, a German businessman and passionate amateur archaeologist named Heinrich Schliemann made an exciting discovery at Mycenae. He unearthed six royal tombs, dating back to around 1600BC, which provided a great step forward in our knowledge of the Mycenaeans, their religious beliefs and way of life.

Pottery figure of a Mycenaean goddess

RELIGION

From the many objects found in the royal tombs, archaeologists concluded that Mycenaean religious beliefs were similar to those of the Minoans. Both cultures seem to have believed in life after death, and rated goddesses more highly than gods.

SHAFT GRAVES

The earliest royal tombs were shaft graves. These are very deep holes in the ground where several bodies, usually from the same family, were buried. The graves could be as deep as 12m (40ft). Objects such as pots and weapons were buried with the dead for use in the afterlife.

This shaft grave is marked by a tombstone above ground.

THOLOS TOMBS

By about 1500BC, beehive-shaped tombs, known as *tholos* tombs, were being used to bury members of the royal family. The dead person was buried with great ceremony, along with valuable possessions, such as weapons and ornaments.

Pausanias, a Greek historian, believed these tombs were treasuries, rather than tombs, because of the magnificence of the things inside. Unfortunately, they were easy to break into, so very few have been found with their treasures intact.

INTERNET LINKS

For a link to a website where you can see photographs of Mycenaean tombs and some of the spectacular treasures found in the tombs, go to **www.usborne-quicklinks.com**

The scene here shows a reconstruction of a funeral procession to a tomb known as the Treasury of Atreus, after a legendary Mycenaean king.

Many of the king's possessions, including his war chariot, were buried with him. Mourners and musicians accompanied the body, and a sheep was led in to be sacrificed.

TOMB TREASURE

Shaft graves were much deeper and more difficult for thieves to rob, and so the treasure buried with the royal families has often survived. The graves at Mycenae were found with all kinds of precious things.

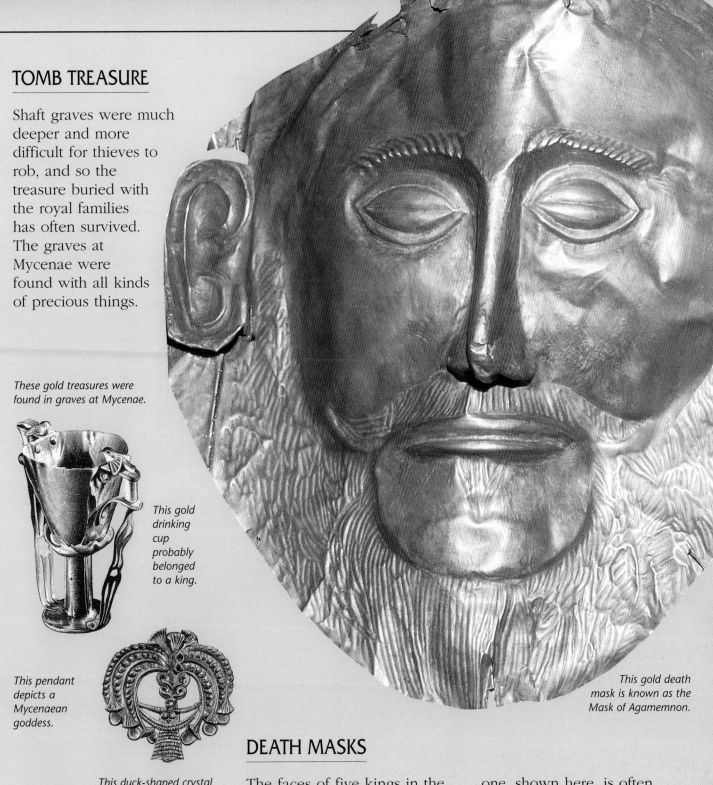

These gold treasures were found in graves at Mycenae.

This gold drinking cup probably belonged to a king.

This pendant depicts a Mycenaean goddess.

This duck-shaped crystal vessel may have been used in religious ceremonies.

This gold death mask is known as the Mask of Agamemnon.

DEATH MASKS

The faces of five kings in the Mycenae burial chambers were covered with masks of gold or electrum (a metal made of gold and silver). To make the mask, the metal was heated, then beaten into shape. Experts believe these masks were attempts at real portraits of the kings. The most famous one, shown here, is often named after Agamemnon, the legendary king in Homer's tale of the Trojan War (see pages 28-29). But, sadly, it can't really be Agamemnon himself. The mask dates back to about 1550BC, but the Trojan War, if it happened, took place later - around 1250BC.

WARRIORS AND TRADERS

Judging from what they left behind, the Mycenaeans seem to have been a very warlike people. Archaeologists have dug up masses of weapons and images of war and battle scenes.

This carved head from Mycenae shows a soldier in a helmet made from boars' tusks.

WARRIOR KINGS

The king of a Mycenaean city was expected to be a warrior too. He had to look after his soldiers, and to supply them with food, housing, land and slaves. This was arranged by officials in the palace, where many of the soldiers lived.

In battle, kings and nobles wore helmets and protective clothing made of bronze. Ordinary soldiers just wore leather tunics.

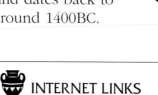

The king leading his soldiers into battle

Nobles rode into battle in chariots. Soldiers marched on foot.

WHAT SOLDIERS WORE

Most of what we know about what the soldiers wore comes from contemporary pictures - although one nearly complete bronze suit was found in a tomb in a place called Dendra (see the map on page 22).

The suit is made of bronze plates. With it was a boars' tusk helmet, some bronze greaves (leg guards), two swords, and the remains of a wooden-framed shield. The whole find dates back to around 1400BC.

INTERNET LINKS

For links to websites where you can see Mycenaean metalwork, weapons and goods from a shipwreck, go to **www.usborne-quicklinks.com**

This soldier's suit was found in a tholos tomb.

Boar's tusk helmet

Bronze high neck guard

Shoulder pieces

Bronze protective clothing, called a cuirass

Bands to protect the stomach and lower body

SHIELDS AND SWORDS

The shields that the Mycenaeans used were made of oxhide stretched over a wooden frame. There were three different shapes. Shields were large and heavy, and warriors carried them into battle slung on their backs.

Shield shaped like the number eight

Tower shield

Round shield

Daggers and swords were made from bronze. Some were highly decorated and look similar to those found on Crete. They may even have been made on the island.

A Mycenaean gold sword hilt. Above is a bronze dagger, inlaid with a scene of a lion hunt.

MEDITERRANEAN TRADERS

Copper from Cyprus

Bronze swords and daggers

Jars of wine and oil

This scene from a Mycenaean port shows traders unloading goods.

The Mycenaeans were great traders. At first, there was fierce competition from the Minoans, but after the Mycenaeans invaded Crete, they took over the Minoan trade for themselves. They had trading posts all along the eastern Mediterranean coast - in Asia Minor (now Turkey) and Lebanon - but they also traded goods from as far away as Scandinavia and Africa.

The Mycenaean world in 1400BC

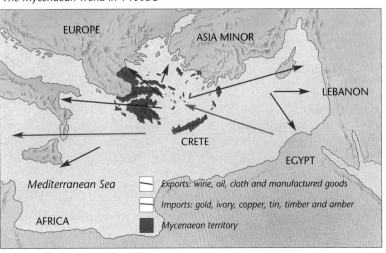

EUROPE

ASIA MINOR

LEBANON

CRETE

EGYPT

Mediterranean Sea

AFRICA

Exports: wine, oil, cloth and manufactured goods

Imports: gold, ivory, copper, tin, timber and amber

Mycenaean territory

TROY AND THE TROJAN WAR

The *Iliad*, an epic poem by Homer, a Greek poet who lived around 800BC, tells of a war between Greece and Troy – a city in Asia Minor (now Turkey). There was a war around 1250BC, but we don't know if it was the same one that Homer described in his poem.

THE LEGEND

Legend has it that the Trojan War was caused by Helen, Princess of Sparta – the most beautiful woman in the world. All the Greek kings wanted to marry her, but her father made them swear to support the man he chose as her husband – Menelaus of Sparta, brother of Agamemnon of Mycenae.

HELEN MEETS PARIS

King Priam of Troy sent some men to Greece to bargain for the return of a Trojan princess who had been kidnapped. Among them was Paris, Priam's son. When Helen and Paris met, they fell in love and ran away together to Troy. Furious, Menelaus and Agamemnon organized a great military expedition to bring Helen back.

THE TROJAN HORSE

For ten years the Greeks laid siege to Troy and a battle raged outside the city walls. At last, the Greek king Odysseus thought of a trick to win the war. He got his men to build a huge wooden horse, which they left outside the city gates. The Greeks then sailed away under cover of darkness.

GREEK VICTORY

The Trojans thought that the horse was a gift to the goddess Athene. They dragged it inside the city, unaware that Greek soldiers were hidden inside it. That night, the Greeks crept out and opened the city gates. The Greek army returned to storm in and destroy the city.

 INTERNET LINKS

For links to websites where you can read about the story and characters of the Trojan War, go to
www.usborne-quicklinks.com

This is a portrait of Helen of Troy, carved in about 1819 by the Italian neoclassical sculptor, Antonio Canova.

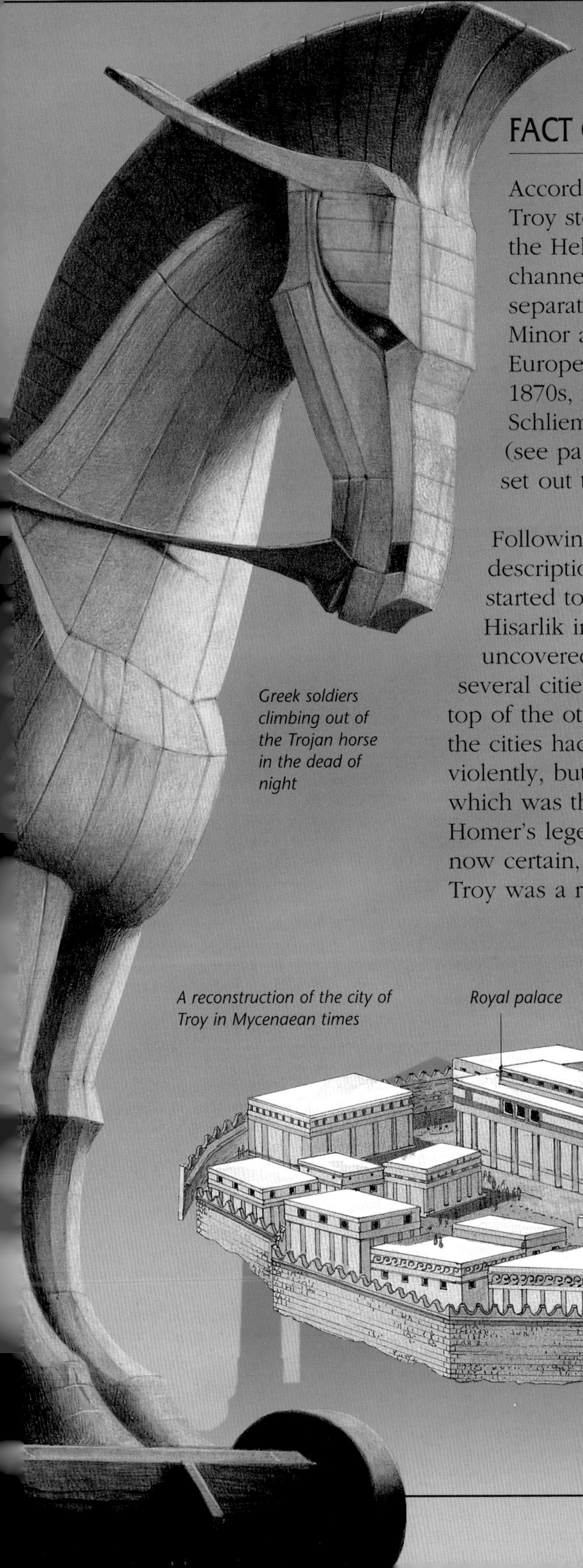

FACT OR FICTION?

According to Homer, Troy stood overlooking the Hellespont – a channel of water that separates Asia Minor and Europe. In the 1870s, Heinrich Schliemann (see page 24) set out to find it.

Following Homer's description, he started to dig at Hisarlik in Turkey, and uncovered the ruins of several cities, built one on top of the other. Several of the cities had been destroyed violently, but it is not clear which was the Troy of Homer's legend. Experts are now certain, though, that Troy was a real place.

PRIAM'S TREASURE

In 1873, Schliemann made an incredible discovery. He found a copper bowl, which turned out to have a hoard of gold, jewels, weapons and ornaments inside. He nicknamed it Priam's Treasure.

This photograph of Schliemann's wife Sophia wearing the jewels was for many years the only record of them that existed.

Although Schliemann believed the treasure to date back to the Trojan War, it was in fact more recent - but it was still a remarkable find, and revealed much about ancient metalworking. It was lost in the chaos at the end of World War Two, but has recently resurfaced in Russia.

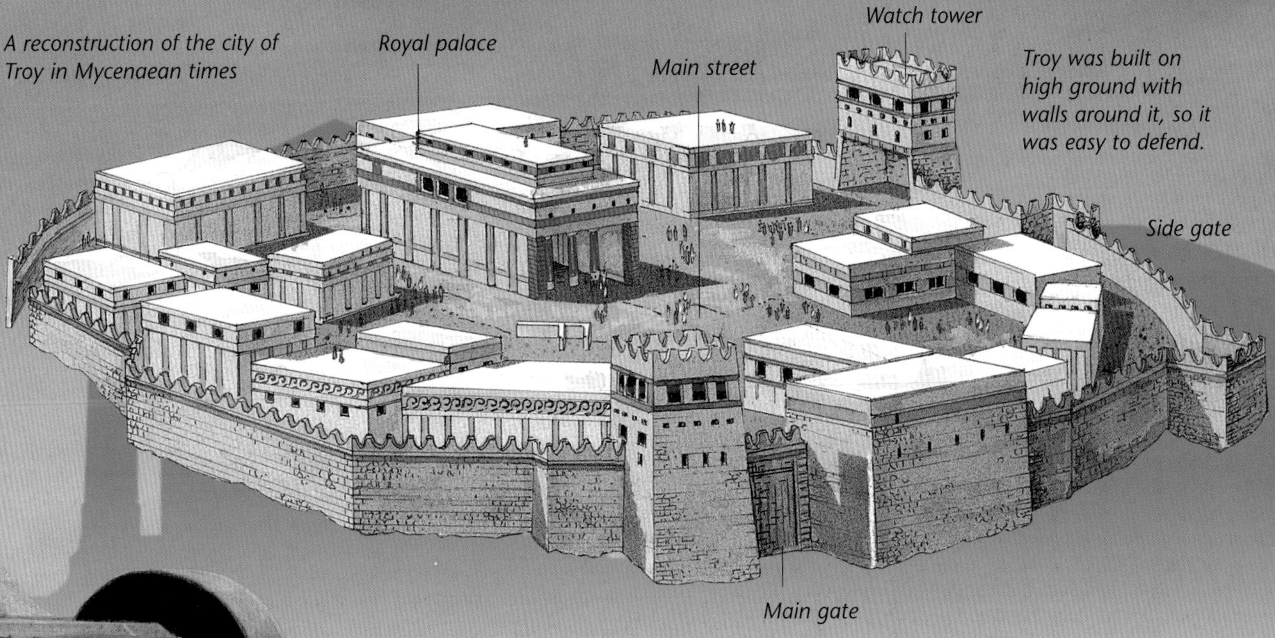

Greek soldiers climbing out of the Trojan horse in the dead of night

A reconstruction of the city of Troy in Mycenaean times

Royal palace

Main street

Watch tower

Troy was built on high ground with walls around it, so it was easy to defend.

Side gate

Main gate

THINGS FALL APART

By around 1200BC, the world of the Mycenaeans was falling apart. Ancient Egyptian records show that, in the second half of the 13th century BC, there was a long run of poor harvests, food shortages and famine in the Mediterranean, which put the whole Mycenaean way of life under threat.

TROUBLED TIMES

During this difficult period, groups of starving Mycenaeans probably attacked each other's cities and villages to steal food and other goods. At around this time, many people built strong defensive walls around their cities, to protect themselves from raiders.

Thick stone walls at the Mycenaean fortress of Tiryns, built in the 11th century BC

THE SEA PEOPLES

In desperation, as their trade and economy disintegrated around them, some groups of Mycenaeans may have gone on raids overseas. This may have been the real cause of the Trojan War, described by Homer in his poem the *Iliad* (see pages 28-29).

Some Greeks may even have been driven away from their homes altogether. There are Egyptian reports of groups of people on the move in the eastern Mediterranean in 1190BC. Some were marching overland, while others set sail in a large fleet of battleships.

This portrait of one of the Sea Peoples was carved on a temple built by the Egyptian pharaoh Ramesses III.

The Egyptians named these migrants the 'Sea Peoples'. Experts don't know exactly who they were or where they were from, but it's possible that some of them may have been Mycenaean refugees.

As they advanced, the Sea Peoples' fleet seized the island of Cyprus. Meanwhile, on land, their army destroyed many cities, and overthrew the powerful Hittite empire in Asia Minor (Turkey).

This reconstruction of a sea battle between Egyptians and Sea Peoples is based on a carving at Luxor in Egypt.

Egyptian ship

Sea Peoples' ship

EGYPT'S VICTORY

The Sea Peoples' army and fleet were decisively defeated by the powerful Egyptian pharaoh Ramesses III. After this final blow, the Sea Peoples scattered over the Mediterranean. Some may have become the ancestors of the Etruscans, who later settled in Italy. Others moved to Sicily, or to Palestine, and became the ancestors of a people known as the Philistines.

THE DORIANS

One by one, the Mycenaean cities were abandoned and destroyed, either by earthquakes or by enemy conquest. Then, a people called the Dorians became dominant in the Peloponnese in southern Greece. They took advantage of the troubles to increase their power.

Dorian Greek
Ionic Greek
Aeolic Greek
Arcadian Greek

ASIA MINOR

Aegean Sea

GREECE

PELOPONNESE

CRETE

This map shows where the main Greek dialects were spoken.

INTERNET LINKS

For a link to a website where you can find out more about the Sea Peoples, go to www.usborne-quicklinks.com

This map shows the different routes taken by the Sea Peoples.

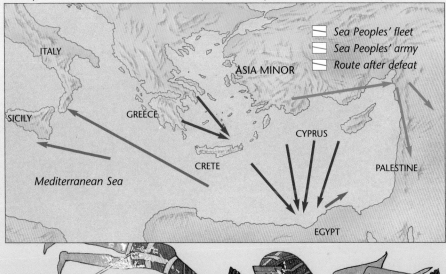

ITALY

ASIA MINOR

Sea Peoples' fleet
Sea Peoples' army
Route after defeat

GREECE

SICILY

CRETE

CYPRUS

PALESTINE

Mediterranean Sea

EGYPT

Wherever the Dorians settled, their dialect took root, and it was from this that the Greek language later developed. But the Dorians did not adopt the artistic skills of the people they conquered, and many of the cultural achievements of the Mycenaeans were lost, including the art of writing.

THE DARK AGES

The period in Greece from 1100 to 800BC is sometimes described as the Dark Ages, as we know very little about what was happening - although new excavations are starting to reveal more. The Greeks lost the art of writing, so they left no written records, and foreigners, such as the Egyptians, hardly mention them either.

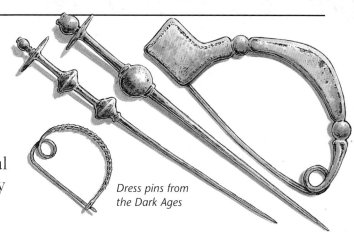

Dress pins from the Dark Ages

GREECE IN DECLINE

By the beginning of this period, the population in Greece had fallen hugely. This was most probably due to the widespread famine and warfare that hit the region at the end of the Mycenaean period. The palaces were destroyed, and a whole way of life crumbled with them. Old styles of metalwork and pottery died out, and skills such as fresco-painting and gem-cutting were forgotten.

DAILY LIFE

Most people were very poor and probably grew just enough to eat. They would have lived in small huts made of mud brick, with thatched roofs. As these materials do not last long, few buildings from this period have survived.

Mud brick house

Vase in the new geometric style that developed in the Dark Ages

EUBOEA

One exception to this picture of poverty was on the large island of Euboea (now called Evia). As early as 900BC, the Euboeans were trading abroad, but wars between the two main cities on the island eventually brought an end to this properous culture.

The island of Euboea

Terracotta centaur from Euboea

A statue of a man carrying a calf from about 570BC, found on the Acropolis in Athens

ARCHAIC GREECE

THE ARCHAIC PERIOD

Sometime after 800BC, Greek culture began to show the first signs of a revival. This new era, which lasted until around 500BC, is known as the Archaic Period. The Greek population grew and there was increasing contact with other lands. Greek art improved and the skill of writing was rediscovered and developed (see page 50).

INTERNET LINKS

For links to websites where you can see an animated map showing the spread of Greek colonies and design a Greek amphora online, go to **www.usborne-quicklinks.com**

This vase, called an amphora, was painted in about 560BC. It is decorated with a scene from a wild boar hunt, which was typical of the style of the time.

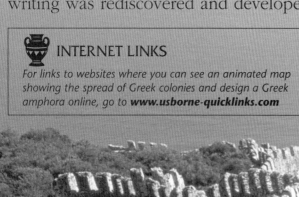

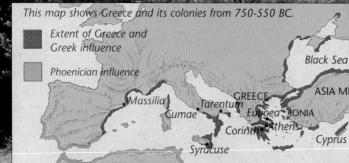

This map shows Greece and its colonies from 750-550 BC.

- Extent of Greece and Greek influence
- Phoenician influence

Massilia
Cumae
Tarentum
GREECE
Euboea
Corinth
Athens
IONIA
Syracuse
Cyprus
Cyrene
Black Sea
ASIA MINOR
PHOENICIA

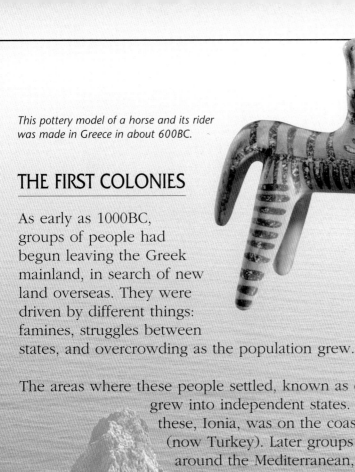

This pottery model of a horse and its rider was made in Greece in about 600BC.

THE FIRST COLONIES

As early as 1000BC, groups of people had begun leaving the Greek mainland, in search of new land overseas. They were driven by different things: famines, struggles between states, and overcrowding as the population grew.

The areas where these people settled, known as colonies, soon grew into independent states. The first of these, Ionia, was on the coast of Asia Minor (now Turkey). Later groups settled all around the Mediterranean, from France to the Black Sea. The colonies were often in places with a natural port and good farmland, where the locals were friendly.

TRADE AND COMMERCE

Trade grew between the Greek cities and their colonies, and with the Phoenicians from the eastern Mediterranean. Merchants sailed from port to port, buying and selling goods. The Greek colonies acted as staging posts for Greek trade with foreign lands.

This photograph shows the ruins of a fortress on the Ionian coast, where the Greeks established their first colonies.

THE GRAIN TRADE

Many of the Greek cities could not grow enough to feed all their people, so grain - mainly barley - was the most crucial import. Athens had to import as much as two-thirds of all its grain from abroad, mostly from Greek colonies around the shores of the Black Sea.

GREEK CITY-STATES

By the Archaic Period, mainland Greece was made up of a cluster of small city-states, politically independent from each other. The word the Greeks used for a city-state was *polis* - which is the origin of our word 'politics'. Although these states were often rivals, and sometimes fought wars against each other, they shared the same Greek identity - a common language, culture and religion - which created strong links between them.

This image from a Greek vase shows an Athenian slave and his owner.

This map shows the city-states in around 500BC. The most powerful cities were Athens, Corinth and Sparta.

WHAT WAS THE CITY-STATE LIKE?

The Greeks liked to keep their political units fairly small - even the largest city-state, Athens, had no more than a few thousand citizens (see opposite page). Each *polis* consisted of a single city, enclosed by walls, and its surrounding countryside. Inside the walls was an area of high ground, called an *acropolis*, and an open area, called an *agora*, which was used for markets and meetings.

FREE MEN AND SLAVES

Greek society was made up of two main groups: free men (and their wives and families) and slaves. Slaves were workers who were owned by free men and had no legal rights. Many lived closely with their owners, like members of the family, but were very rarely granted their freedom.

WHO RULED?

At the beginning of the Archaic Period, most Greek states were governed by groups of rich landowners, called aristocrats. This kind of government is known as an aristocracy, which means 'rule by the important people'. Sometimes, if they were unpopular, the aristocrats chose respected, important men to rule instead. This is called an oligarchy, which means 'rule by the few'.

As trading activities increased, a middle class of merchants and craftsmen began to prosper. They resented the aristocracy and demanded a role in politics. This often led to riots between different social groups.

THE TIME OF TYRANTS

To bring peace, the people were sometimes prepared to let one very powerful man rule alone. This sort of leader was known as a tyrant.

In 621BC, the people of Athens appointed a man called Draco to lead them. He drew up a set of very severe laws. Even minor crimes, such as stealing food, were punished by death.

INTERNET LINKS

For a link to a website where you can find out more about the city-state of Corinth and choose which kind of ruler you would have preferred, go to **www.usborne-quicklinks.com**

SOLON THE REFORMER

Solon

In 594BC, an aristrocrat named Solon was given power and introduced popular reforms. He provided food for the poor, stopped people who owed money from being sold as slaves, and gave citizens a say in the city's affairs. But this didn't satisfy everyone. Solon was forced to leave Athens and unrest broke out again. Then, in 508BC, an aristocrat named Cleisthenes came to power, introducing a radical new system of government, known as democracy (see pages 56-57).

CITIZENS AND METICS

In Athens, free men were eventually divided into two groups: citizens, which meant men who were born in Athens, and metics, who were not.

Citizens could take part in politics, but they were also expected to serve in the army, act as officials and volunteer for jury service. Metics had to pay tax and serve in the army, but they could not own property or get involved in politics.

Metics often worked as craftsmen. This scene from a painted pot shows a cobbler.

SPARTA – A WARRIOR STATE

In the 10th century BC, a group of Dorians settled in Sparta, in Laconia, southern Greece, which became the nucleus of a thriving state. The Spartans soon acquired a reputation for toughness and military strength. After overpowering the local people, they extended their frontiers by conquering nearby Messenia in 740-720BC. Sparta was now one of the largest Greek states of its day.

This Spartan cup, made around 560BC, shows a busy North African trading scene. Not much pottery now survives from Sparta.

The Spartans themselves produced fine metalware and vases, and were also said to have played a role in the development of Greek music.

Map showing Sparta and Argos

This bronze figure shows a Spartan warrior of the 5th century BC.

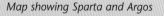

Unlike other states, the Spartans were slow to adopt coins as currency. Instead they used these iron rods.

TRADE AND PROSPERITY

Not only was Sparta one of the largest states, it also had enough fertile land to make it self-sufficient in food. At the start of the Archaic Period, the Spartans were trading with other Greek states, importing luxury goods, such as ivory, amber and cloth.

SPARTA WEAKENED

Their early success was not to last. In 668BC, they were defeated in a war against Argos, another local state. In 630BC, the Messenians began a revolt which dragged on for 17 years. This convinced the Spartans they must make drastic changes - both to keep the population under control and to protect themselves from foreign invasions.

SPARTAN SOCIETY

People who lived in Sparta belonged to distinct social classes. For instance, only men (and not women) who were born in the city of Sparta were regarded as citizens. Citizens all served in the army and could vote on important issues in an assembly. There were only ever around 9,000 citizens at any one time, and outsiders were never allowed to join their ranks.

The descendants of the people who had surrendered to Spartan rule were known as *perioikoi*. Although they were not Spartan citizens, they were free and were allowed to trade and join the army.

Descendants of people who had resisted Spartan rule were known as *helots*, and forced to work on the land - more or less as slaves. They were made to surrender most of their crops to their Spartan masters. Although there were many more helots than Spartans, the Spartans made sure they had no power - and no chance to rebel.

These helots are gathering crops, while a Spartan soldier watches over them.

A SOLDIER STATE

The Spartans' solution was to set themselves up as a first-class military state. Every man had to become a full-time soldier and devote his life to training and fighting. All Spartans lived very hard lives, and had little contact with the outside world.

This huge bronze pot, as tall as a man, was made in Sparta in the 6th century BC. It was found in the grave of a Celtic ruler at Vix in France.

The handles are shaped like mythological beasts called gorgons.

The rim is decorated with a scene showing hoplites and horse-drawn chariots.

GREEK ARMIES

Cavalry soldier

At the beginning of the Archaic Period, the most important part of any Greek army was the cavalry - the soldiers on horseback. Soldiers had to provide their own horses and weapons, so early armies were dominated by rich men who could afford to do this.

Auxiliary soldiers

FOOT SOLDIERS

In these early times, foot soldiers tended to be fairly poor, so their weapons and equipment were poor as well. By the 7th century BC, however, there was a new elite class of foot soldiers, called hoplites, who were better equipped and better trained (see pages 42-43). Once the hoplites had grown in importance, cavalry units became smaller.

AUXILIARIES

Poor men who could not afford the full battle kit and weapons of a hoplite soldier usually served instead in lightly armed auxiliary units. These units included archers, stone slingers, and men called *psiloi*, who were armed with clubs and stones.

SIEGE WARFARE

In wartime, a common tactic was to lay siege to a city by surrounding it - even going to the lengths of building walls around it. The idea was to starve the city into submission - although this could take months. In 305-304BC, the city of Rhodes managed to hold out for a year against the Macedonian army, which was eventually forced to withdraw.

INTERNET LINKS

For links to websites where you can examine battle scenes on a Greek pot, and see pictures of Greek weapons, go to **www.usborne-quicklinks.com**

A trumpeter blares out to encourage the attackers and give orders.

These soldiers are swinging a battering ram, suspended on ropes to help the swinging action.

An archer

A stone slinger

SIEGE WEAPONS

Another tactic was for the army to try to storm the city and take it by force. By about 400BC, the Greeks were using a heavy wooden beam, called a battering ram, to smash into walls or gates. The ram was attached to ropes inside a wooden covering, and was moved back and forth by a team of men.

The attacking army also used siege towers – huge wooden structures that could be moved up against the city walls, as platforms for attack.

Hoplites in formation, ready to storm the city

Attackers climb up the tower, so they can clamber onto the city walls.

Defenders throw rocks and spears and shoot arrows.

Towers were sometimes divided into floors.

Each level housed archers or a catapult.

A catapult could fire arrows or javelins.

The main body of the battering ram was made of wood.

The battering ram took its name from the bronze ram-shaped head.

HOPLITES

By the 7th century BC, foot soldiers called hoplites were the elite corps of any Greek army. Hoplites all used similar clothing and weapons, but most armies did not have a special uniform.

EQUIPMENT

To protect his body, a hoplite wore a joined breast and back plate known as a cuirass. Early models were made from two bronze plates, attached with leather straps at the side.

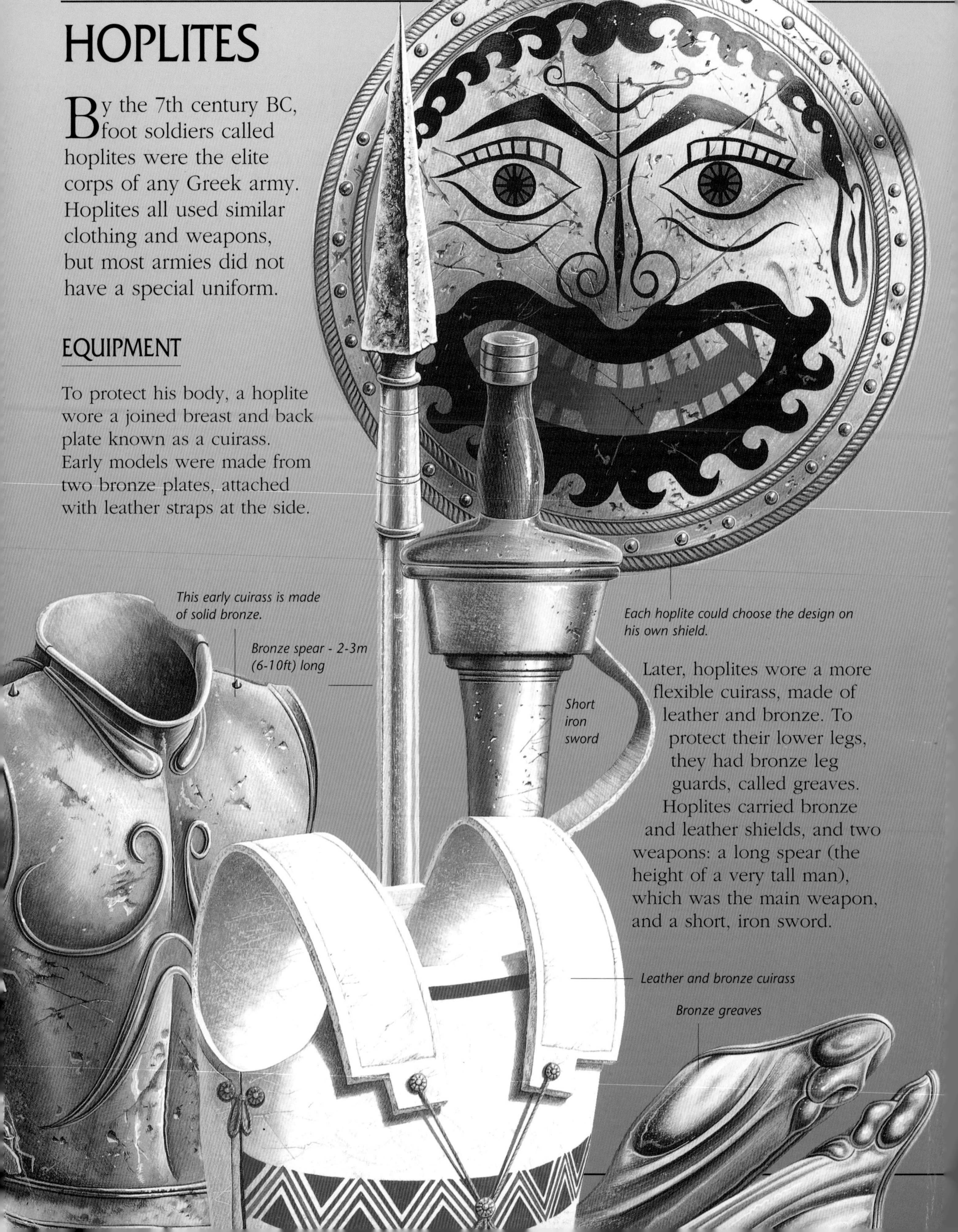

This early cuirass is made of solid bronze.

Bronze spear - 2-3m (6-10ft) long

Short iron sword

Each hoplite could choose the design on his own shield.

Later, hoplites wore a more flexible cuirass, made of leather and bronze. To protect their lower legs, they had bronze leg guards, called greaves. Hoplites carried bronze and leather shields, and two weapons: a long spear (the height of a very tall man), which was the main weapon, and a short, iron sword.

Leather and bronze cuirass

Bronze greaves

HELMETS

Helmets were made of bronze and often had horsehair crests on top. Designs changed over the years: here are just a few of them.

Kegel

The most basic kinds were the Kegel and the Corinthian, both worn in the 7th century BC. Different types evolved from these, one of which was the Illyrian helmet.

Corinthian

Illyrian

The basic Corinthian helmet developed into one with ear holes, so that soldiers could hear better in battle. The Chalcidian helmet left both the ears and the mouth uncovered.

Later Corinthian

Between the 5th and the 2nd centuries BC, the Thracian helmet became popular. It had a peak at the front and long cheek pieces.

Chalcidian

Thracian

A phalanx charging forward in battle

BATTLE FORMATION

Rather than battling in one-to-one combat, as warriors had done in earlier times, hoplites fought in an organized formation called a phalanx. The phalanx was a long block of soldiers, usually eight ranks deep. Each man was protected partly by his own shield and partly by the shield of the soldier on his right hand side.

The man on the far right was left partly exposed. Because of this, the right wing of a phalanx was vulnerable. In battle, a general would often try to attack the enemy on this weak side.

ATTACK

In attack, a phalanx charged forward so that the full weight of men and shields smashed into the enemy. The two opposing phalanxes would then push against each other until one gave way.

This hoplite soldier was painted on a Greek plate, dated around 560BC.

 INTERNET LINKS

For a link to a website where you can find out lots about the weapons of the Greek hoplite, go to www.usborne-quicklinks.com

GREEK WARSHIPS

The most powerful and famous warship in the ancient world was a Greek design known as a trireme. As Greek cities grew rich and powerful, they built fleets of triremes to patrol the eastern Mediterranean and wage war on their enemies.

A MODERN TRIREME

In 1985, a group of ship-lovers from all over the world constructed a full-size replica trireme, named *Olympias*. Building the ship taught them a lot about the design of these ancient warships. During sea trials, the team discovered more about how the ship and crew performed. *Olympias* is now on permanent display at Neon Faliron, near the port of Piraeus in Greece.

This Athenian carving of a trireme dates back to around 400BC.

This photograph shows a modern Greek trireme, called Olympias, in full sail.

Triremes were expensive to build. In ancient times, only the richest cities, such as Athens and Corinth, could afford to commission many of them.

FAST AND FIERCE

Triremes were formidable in battle, because they were fast and easy to steer. Although they had sails, they always put them away and rowed into battle, because it was easier to start, stop and turn. The oarsmen propelled the ship through the water at up to 15km (9 miles) an hour – much faster than it could move under sail.

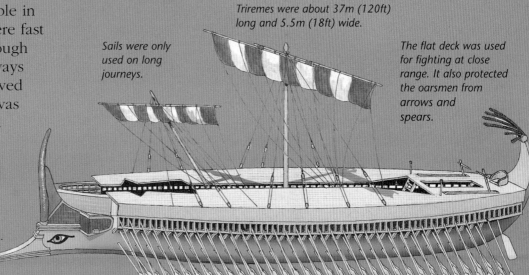

Triremes were about 37m (120ft) long and 5.5m (18ft) wide.

Sails were only used on long journeys.

The flat deck was used for fighting at close range. It also protected the oarsmen from arrows and spears.

The wooden ram was 2m (6.5ft) long and covered in bronze, to punch holes in enemy ships.

There were three tiers of long oars inside the hull.

Two huge oars at the back were used for steering.

THE CREW

Triremes carried crews of up to 200 men, most of whom were oarsmen. The name trireme came from the Latin for 'three oars', because the men sat on three levels inside the hull. Also on board were naval officers, soldiers, archers and deckhands.

 INTERNET LINKS

For links to websites where you can see photos of replica Greek triremes and command a trireme online, go to **www.usborne-quicklinks.com**

The upper rowers, called thranites, sat in two rows of 31.

The middle rowers were called zygites. They sat in two rows of 27.

The bottom rowers were called thalamites. They also sat in two rows of 27.

BATTLE TACTICS

At the start of battle, enemies often faced each other in two long lines. The main tactic was to attempt to ram an enemy ship and sink or disable it.

The best places to aim for were the back and sides of an enemy ship. Four different ways of doing this are described below.

1 *Sweep around the far end of the line and attack from behind.*

2 *Swerve away from the opponent at the last moment, pull the oars on board and then sweep past the enemy ship, breaking its oars.*

3 *Make for a gap in the line and then veer to the side at the last moment, smashing into the side of the enemy.*

4 *Dart through a gap in the line, wheel around and attack the enemy from behind.*

THE PERSIAN WARS

In the 6th century BC, the rising stars on the scene in western Asia were the Persians. As they carved out an empire for themselves, they sparked a series of clashes with the Greek city-states, which lasted for over 50 years.

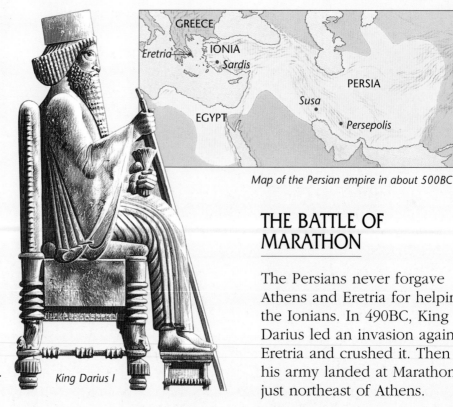

King Darius I

Map of the Persian empire in about 500BC

WHO WERE THE PERSIANS?

The Persians were a people from a small kingdom called Persia, at the heart of the country which is now Iran. Their expansion took off in 550BC, when they conquered the nearby kingdom of Media. By 485BC, under Darius I, they had built up a vast empire - one of the largest and most powerful in the ancient world.

Conflict with the Greeks first looked likely in 546BC, when the Persians succeeded in conquering the Greek states in Ionia, on the western coast of Asia Minor, in the area which is now Turkey.

At first, the Greek city-states did little to protest, until 500-499BC, when the Ionians rebelled. This time, they were backed by Athens and Eretria, who provided both men and ships. The Greeks destroyed the Persian city of Sardis, but the revolt collapsed when the Athenians and Eretrians withdrew their support.

THE BATTLE OF MARATHON

The Persians never forgave Athens and Eretria for helping the Ionians. In 490BC, King Darius led an invasion against Eretria and crushed it. Then his army landed at Marathon, just northeast of Athens.

The Athenians and their allies marched an army of 10,000 men to meet them. Although the Greeks were heavily outnumbered, they won a tremendous victory, by means of superior tactics and the strength of the hoplite phalanx (see page 43).

A runner was sent to Athens, 25 miles away, with the news. Right after announcing it, he dropped dead from exhaustion. Modern marathon races are named after this.

Persian relief from the palace at Persepolis, seat of the Persian kings

The first marathon runner

THE SECOND INVASION

King Darius I died soon after the Battle of Marathon, but memories of the Persian defeat festered in the mind of his son, King Xerxes. In 480BC, Xerxes led another invasion into Greek territory - this time overland. To cross the Hellespont, a thin stretch of water separating Europe and Asia, Xerxes had his engineers construct two huge bridges, entirely from ships.

The first confrontation took place in a narrow mountain pass called Thermopylae. At first, a small army of Greeks was able to hold back the Persian advance. But a Greek traitor showed the Persians a secret route around the pass.

Realizing there was no way out, Leonidas, the Spartan commander, stayed on with a small force to fight and be slaughtered, allowing the rest of the Greek army to flee to safety. It was one of the greatest, and most famous, gestures of self-sacrifice in ancient history.

The Persians then marched on an undefended Athens. Excited by their victory, they ran riot in the city, and looted and set fire to the Acropolis.

This monument at Thermopylae is to Leonidas, the Spartan commander who led the Greek army in the battle there.

This is a reconstruction of one of the boat bridges built by the Persians across the Hellespont.

The bridges built by the Persians were made up of more than 600 ships.

The huge Persian army was said to have taken seven days to march across.

THE DECLINE OF PERSIA

The destruction of Athens marked a low point for the Greeks in their conflict with Persia. However, while the Persians were celebrating their victory on land, trouble was brewing for them at sea.

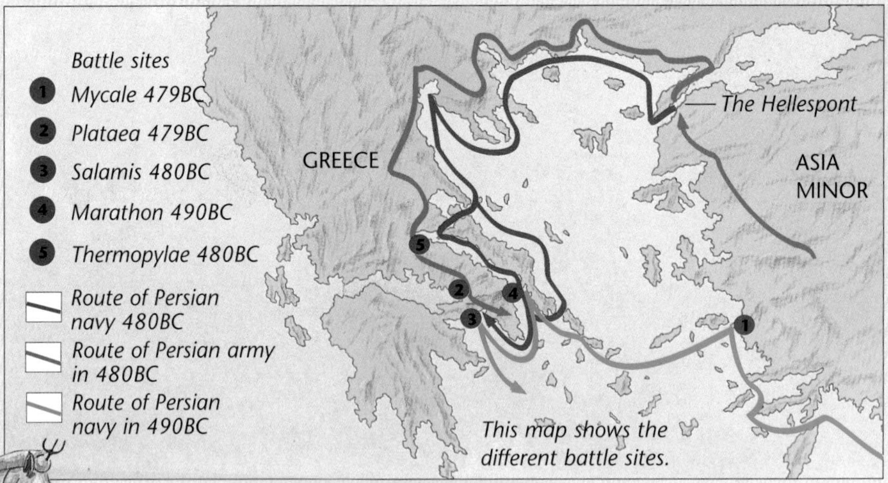

Battle sites

1. Mycale 479BC
2. Plataea 479BC
3. Salamis 480BC
4. Marathon 490BC
5. Thermopylae 480BC

Route of Persian navy 480BC

Route of Persian army in 480BC

Route of Persian navy in 490BC

GREECE

The Hellespont

ASIA MINOR

This map shows the different battle sites.

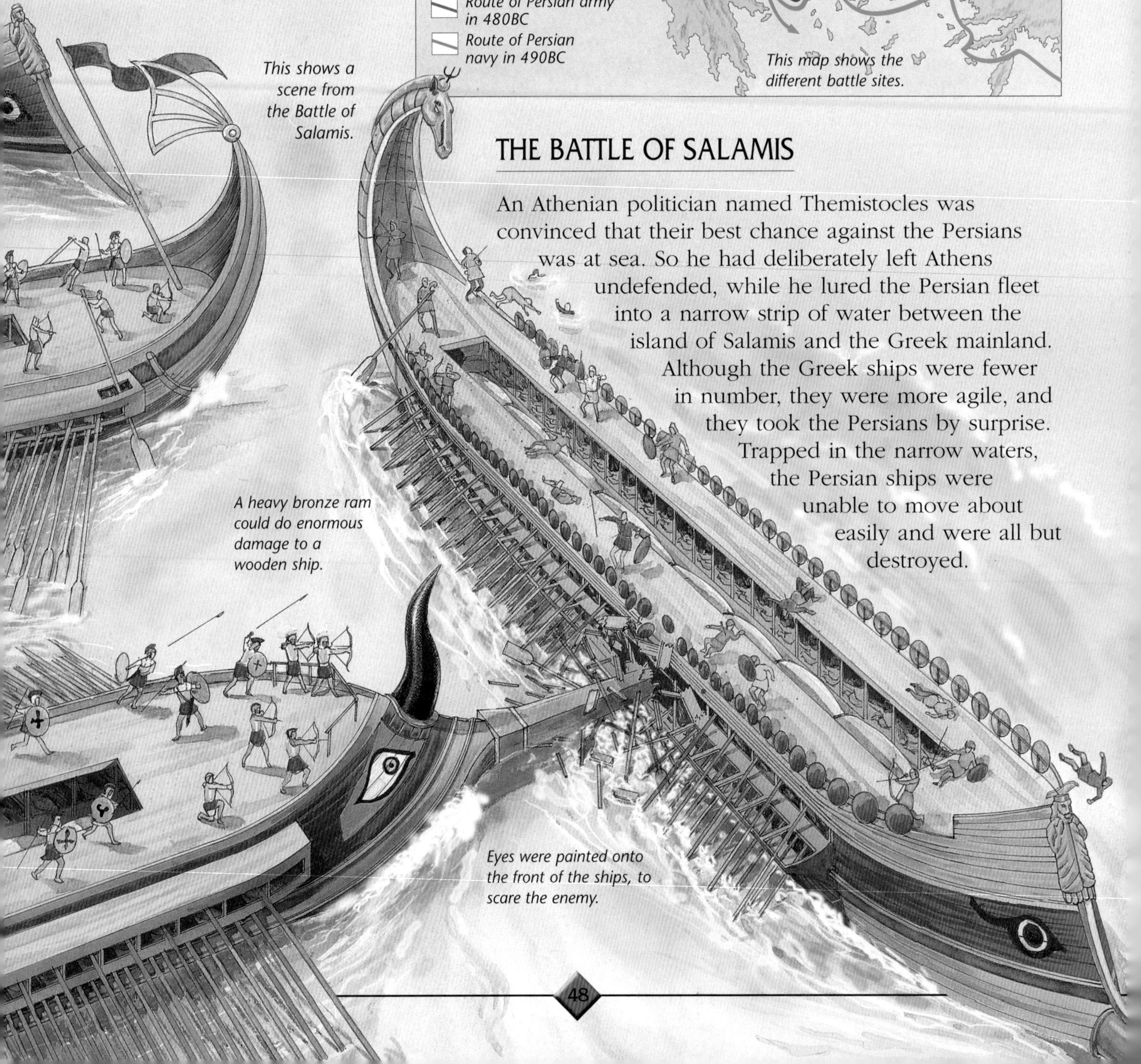

This shows a scene from the Battle of Salamis.

THE BATTLE OF SALAMIS

An Athenian politician named Themistocles was convinced that their best chance against the Persians was at sea. So he had deliberately left Athens undefended, while he lured the Persian fleet into a narrow strip of water between the island of Salamis and the Greek mainland. Although the Greek ships were fewer in number, they were more agile, and they took the Persians by surprise. Trapped in the narrow waters, the Persian ships were unable to move about easily and were all but destroyed.

A heavy bronze ram could do enormous damage to a wooden ship.

Eyes were painted onto the front of the ships, to scare the enemy.

THE INVASION ENDS

In 479BC, the Greeks amassed an enormous army, led by the Spartan general Pausanias, and defeated the Persians on land at a place called Plataea. Meanwhile, Greek forces attacked and burned the entire Persian fleet while it was moored at Mycale, off the coast of Asia Minor. The Persian invasion was finally over.

MEETING ON DELOS

Most Greeks believed it was only a matter of time before the Persians struck again - and they wanted to be ready for an attack. In 478BC, representatives from Athens and allied states gathered together on the Aegean island of Delos to discuss the problem. There they formed the Delian League, an alliance against any future Persian aggression. Members promised ships and money, to defend each other's territories in times of war.

This painting of one of the Persian elite warriors, known as the Immortals, is taken from the palace at Susa, Persia.

Map showing Delos and the Delian League

GREECE

ASIA MINOR

Athens   *Delos*

League members

WAR IS OVER

After this, the Greeks and the Persians continued to squabble over various territories in the Mediterranean. Egypt, Cyprus and Ionia all became battlegrounds in the struggle between the two powers. Then, in 449BC, the Greeks and the Persians made peace at last.

PERSIA FALLS

By this time, however, the Persian empire was already sliding into decline. King Xerxes had been murdered in 465BC, and his successors were weak, making the empire unstable. Greek power grew as Persian power waned.

King Xerxes taken from a Greek vase dated 330BC

By 330BC, the once all-powerful Persian empire had been overrun by the next great conqueror of the ancient world - Alexander the Great, the king of Macedonia (see pages 106-107).

THE BIRTH OF LITERACY

The skills of reading and writing first developed in Mesopotamia (in modern Iraq) and Egypt, before 3000BC. Literacy helped civilizations to develop because it allowed rulers to keep records and pass messages, helping them to organize large societies and develop trading links with other peoples.

This Greek inscription comes from a memorial stone beside the Sacred Way at Delphi, Greece.

THE GREEK ALPHABET

After the Mycenaean age, the art of writing was lost in Greece. Later, around 800BC, the Greeks adapted an alphabet used by the Phoenicians, a trading people from the eastern Mediterranean. The new script contained fewer letters than previous scripts, which made it much easier to learn. It also included vowels, which made it clearer to read. All modern European alphabets - Roman, Greek and Russian - developed from this Ancient Greek one.

THE SPOKEN WORD

Before the spread of literacy, stories and information about the past were passed down by word of mouth. Professional poets, known as bards, journeyed widely throughout Greece, passing on stories of the gods and Mycenaean heroes.

HOMER

Little is known about Homer's life, although tradition relates that he was blind. His poems were probably written down in his lifetime, or soon after his death, but we don't know exactly how.

The most famous bard was Homer, whose epic poems, the *Iliad* and the *Odyssey*, retold the traditional tales of the Trojan War. Composed between 850BC and 750BC, they are the earliest surviving examples of Greek literature.

 INTERNET LINKS

For links to websites where you can learn how to speak like an ancient Greek and translate Greek names in an online game, go to www.usborne-quicklinks.com

Left: some of the letters from the new Greek alphabet

This Roman bust of Homer is based on a Greek original.

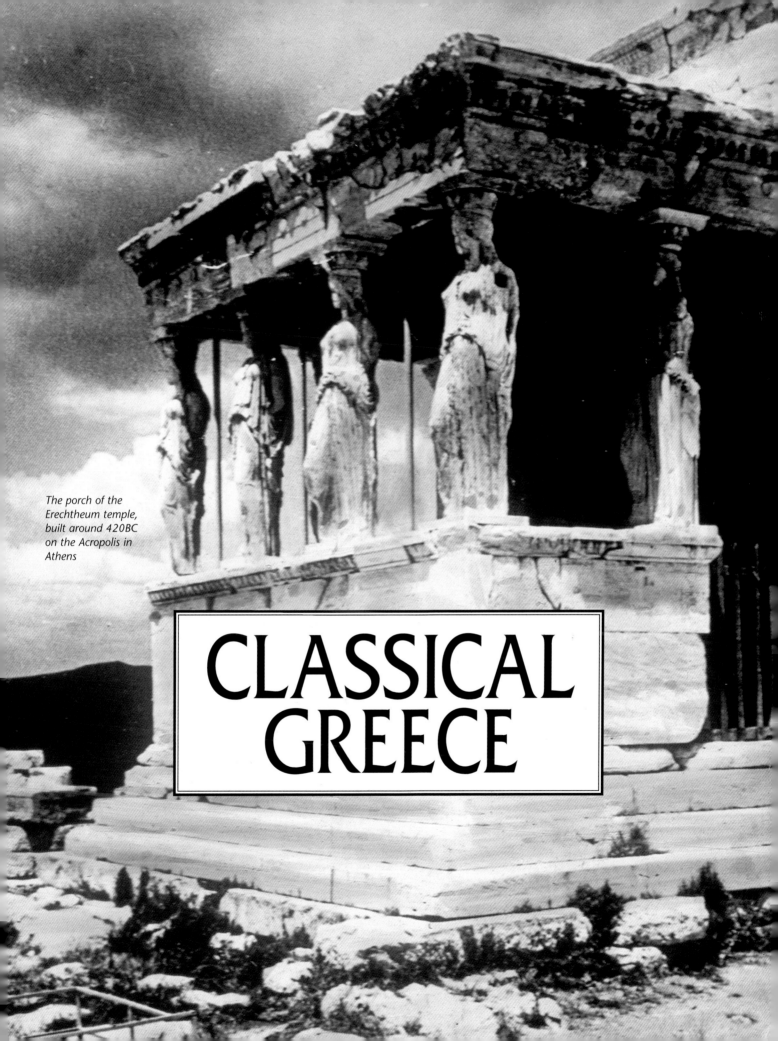

The porch of the
Erechtheum temple,
built around 420BC
on the Acropolis in
Athens

CLASSICAL GREECE

THE GOLDEN AGE OF ATHENS

This period from about 500 to 336BC is known as the Classical period in Greek history. For much of this time, the city-states were dominated by the great city of Athens.

CITY OF CULTURE

Athens prospered in the years of peace following the end of the Persian Wars. The city was magnificently rebuilt, and became the focus for business and culture. At its peak - from about 479 to 431BC - Athens attracted the best artists and scholars of the time. They developed ideas about art, architecture, literature, politics, philosophy, science and history that laid the basis for modern European civilization.

THE EARLY YEARS

The earliest settlement, known as the Acropolis, or "high city", was built high on a rocky hill. The first Athenians settled there because it was easy to defend and there was a freshwater spring.

INTERNET LINKS

For links to websites where you can explore ancient Athens with an interactive map and discover what it was like to live there, go to www.usborne-quicklinks.com

NAMING THE CITY

According to legend, Poseidon, god of the seas, and Athene, goddess of wisdom and war, fought over the naming of the greatest city in Greece. Poseidon promised the people riches through trade, but Athene planted an olive tree. The people decided that this was the more valuable gift, so the city was named Athens after her.

This is a reconstruction of Athens in Classical times. There were probably about a quarter of a million people in the city and surrounding countryside.

Athene's olive tree, from a Greek vase painting

The area around the olive tree on the Acropolis became a sacred place. Later, when the city grew, people built their homes around the base of the hill, reserving the Acropolis for temples and shrines.

At the heart of Athens lay the Agora, the main meeting area in the city. It was a large, open marketplace, surrounded by buildings called stoae containing shops.

Market stalls

Acropolis

The main route from the city up to the Acropolis was called the Panathenaic Way. This was used during a festival called the Panathenaea (see page 98).

The Court of Justice was situated on a hill called the Areopagus. It was named after Ares, the god of war, who was believed to have been tried there for murder.

Carving of Athene, goddess of Athens

The leaders of the city council held their meetings in this building, called the Tholos.

This is the Bouleuterion, where the city council held its meetings.

Behind the Bouleuterion was a temple dedicated to Hephaestos, god of metalsmiths and craftsmen. It was also known as the Theseum, after the hero Theseus.

Many craftsmen lived in these houses near the Agora.

53

THE ACROPOLIS

Towering over the ancient city of Athens was the Acropolis, or 'high city', the site of all the main temples to the gods. In 449BC, Pericles, the political leader of Athens, began a massive rebuilding of the Acropolis, to repair the damage done by the Persians.

This Roman copy of the statue of Athene from the Parthenon is made of unpainted marble. The original was made of wood and ivory, covered with gold.

THE PARTHENON

The main temple on the Acropolis, the Parthenon, was dedicated to Athene, patron goddess of Athens. It was designed by an architect named Ictinus and constructed of white marble, brightly painted. Although it is now in ruins, with few sculptures and no paint left in place, it is still one of the most famous buildings in the world.

TRICKS OF THE EYE

Looking at the columns of a temple can play funny tricks on the eye. From below, a column with absolutely straight sides can look thinner in the middle - even though it's not. So Greek architects designed their columns to bulge slightly in the middle.

 **INTERNET LINKS**

For links to websites where you can explore the main temples of the Acropolis, including the Parthenon, with panoramic movies, go to **www.usborne-quicklinks.com**

THE GOLDEN STATUE

There were statues of Athene - portrayed in her different roles - all over the Acropolis. The most magnificent, and expensive, was probably the enormous statue of Athene Parthenos (Athene the Virgin), that stood just inside the Parthenon. About 12m (40ft) high, it was made of wood and ivory, with robes of pure gold, which were removed whenever there was a risk of the city being attacked. The statue is said to have cost more to make than the Parthenon itself.

This is a reconstruction of the Parthenon, as it would have looked when newly built.

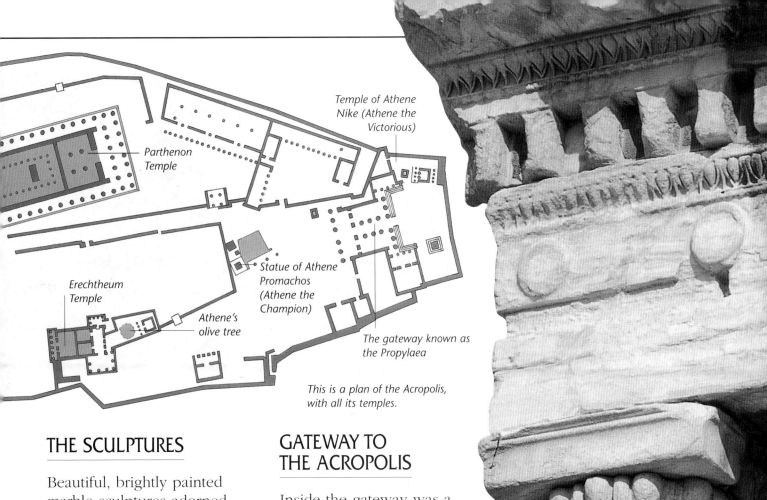

Temple of Athene
Nike (Athene the
Victorious)

Parthenon
Temple

Erechtheum
Temple

Statue of Athene
Promachos
(Athene the
Champion)

Athene's
olive tree

The gateway known as
the Propylaea

*This is a plan of the Acropolis,
with all its temples.*

THE SCULPTURES

Beautiful, brightly painted
marble sculptures adorned
the outside of the Parthenon.
They were designed by
Pheidias, one of the greatest
artists of the 5th century BC.

*These horsemen are part of the carved
frieze on the outside of the Parthenon.
The paint has long since worn away.*

The carvings formed a
horizontal band, or frieze,
showing scenes from Athene's
life, and from other Greek
legends, such as the struggle
between good and evil.

GATEWAY TO
THE ACROPOLIS

Inside the gateway was a
gallery of paintings and a
huge bronze statue to Athene
Promachos (Athene the
Champion). Nearby, on the
Acropolis walls, was a small temple
dedicated to Athene Nike (Athene
the Victorious), which was carved
with scenes telling the story of the
Trojan War (see pages 28-29).

ATHENE'S CONTEST
WITH POSEIDON

On the site of Athene's legendary
contest with Poseidon (see page
52) was the Erectheum temple,
named after Erechtheus, a
mythical king of Athens from
Mycenaean times. Athene's
olive tree grew in the
courtyard, and six graceful
statues of young women,
known as caryatids,
decorated the side porch.

*This is one
of the caryatids
from the porch of
the Erechtheum.*

THE FIRST DEMOCRATIC STATES

At the end of the Archaic Period, some Greek cities overthrew their tyrants and replaced them with a radical new form of government. The new system - which provided a model for political systems in the modern world - is called democracy, from the Greek words *demos* (people), and *kratos* (rule). Unlike modern democracies, though, only citizens had a say. Women, slaves and men born outside the city were all excluded.

THE ATHENIAN MODEL

The Athenian system was introduced in 508BC, by an aristocrat named Cleisthenes. He set up an Assembly, where every citizen could speak and vote. It met every 10 days, on a hill called the Pnyx, and debated proposals made by the Council (see opposite).

The Assembly required 600 citizens for a meeting to take place. If there were too few people, police were sent to round up more.

PERICLES

Pericles was an enormously popular politician in Athens. He dominated the political scene from around 443BC, and was responsible for rebuilding the Acropolis. He was elected *strategos* (see opposite) nearly every year, until his death in 429BC.

INTERNET LINKS

For a link to a website where you can find out lots more and watch short films about Pericles and Cleisthenes, go to
www.usborne-quicklinks.com

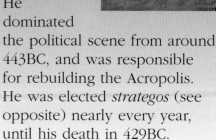

This 19th-century painting shows a man making a speech at the funeral of Pericles.

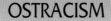

THE OFFICIALS

The people of Athens were divided up into 10 tribes. The Council was made up of 500 citizens - 50 elected from each tribe. The tribes took turns running the Council and the daily affairs of the state.

Under the democratic system, the most important officials were the *strategoi* who were 10 military commanders, elected annually, one from each tribe. Popular *strategoi*, like Pericles, were reelected many times.

There were also 9 archons, also chosen annually, but their duties were mostly ceremonial rather than political. Three of them, shown below, had special roles in the government of Athens.

The Basileus Archon presided over the law courts, arranged religious sacrifices and the renting of temple land, and supervised festivals and feasts.

The Eponymous Archon chose the men who financed the choral and drama contests. He was also responsible for lawsuits about inheritance and the affairs of heiresses, orphans and widows.

The Polemarch Archon was in charge of athletic contests held to commemorate men killed in battle. He also dealt with the legal affairs of metics.

OSTRACISM

The Athenians had an interesting system for getting rid of unpopular politicians. A vote was held once a year, at which any citizen could write down the name of a politician he wished to see banished on a piece of broken pot called an *ostrakon* (plural: *ostraka*). If more than 600 votes were cast against someone, that person would have to leave Athens for 10 years. This procedure is known as ostracism, after the pottery on which the name was written.

These ostraka show the names of two Athenian soldiers and politicians, Aristeides and Cimon. They were both ostracized, and then later recalled to help out in wartime.

THE LAW

One of the duties of an Athenian citizen was to take part in the legal system, because there were no professional lawyers. All citizens over 30 were expected to volunteer for jury service. Each jury had over 200 men, which made it too difficult to bribe or intimidate all the jurors.

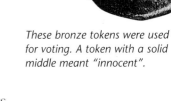

These bronze tokens were used for voting. A token with a solid middle meant "innocent".

A token with a hollow middle meant "guilty".

Citizens had to conduct their own cases, but they could hire speechwriters to help out. Metics (see page 37) could not speak in court. They had to ask a citizen to speak for them.

LIFE IN SPARTA

By the Classical Period, Sparta had become the strongest military power in Greece: its soldiers were celebrated for their bravery throughout the Greek world. But because the Spartans concentrated their efforts on military superiority, the artistic life of the people never had a chance to develop. Artists and philosophers were actively discouraged.

A bronze figure of a Spartan girl, dated around 530BC.

Spartan girls competed in athletic events, wearing short tunics. This shocked the Athenians, who didn't let women take part in sports.

HEALTH AND FITNESS

The Spartans valued good health and physical strength above all else, because all the men were destined to become soldiers. Each new baby was examined by officials and, if it showed signs of weakness, it was left outside to die. Women were expected to keep fit by training in athletic events, so that they would give birth to healthy babies.

This misty and mountainous landscape is at Mistra in Sparta.

A SOLDIER'S LIFE

Many Spartan sculptures, like this bronze figure, depict warriors.

Until the age of 20, boys were educated by the state. Then they had to join the army and were elected to one of Sparta's military clubs. Soldiers lived, ate and slept at the club's barracks - where life was cold, hard and uncomfortable. Men did not usually marry until they were 30 and, even then, were very rarely allowed to go home to see their families.

All soldiers were given land, and helots to work it, by the state. This left them free to devote themselves to the army. Part of the produce that came from their land was kept to support the soldiers' families. The rest went to the barracks to feed the soldiers.

GOVERNMENT IN SPARTA

The Spartan government included two kings, a council of elders, and an Assembly. According to legend, a man called Lycurgus established the Spartan laws and system of government, although experts are unsure whether or not he was a real historical character.

KINGS AND OVERSEERS

Sparta's two kings belonged to the two most important families, called the Agiads and the Eurypontids. They always ruled together and led the army in war, but at home their powers were strictly limited to religious duties. The actual running of the state was carried out by five ephors, or overseers, who were elected every year.

THE COUNCIL

The Council, or *gerousia*, consisted of the two kings and 28 council members. These were men over the age of 60 who were elected for life. They drew up the laws, acted as judges, and decided what policies the state should adopt.

THE ASSEMBLY

The Council's proposals had to be passed by the Assembly, or *apella*, which was made up of all citizens over 30. Experts think that the Assembly probably could not debate or amend anything: they could only vote for or against measures. They did this by shouting "yes" or "no", and the loudest group won.

This photograph shows a man dressed as a Spartan warrior at a Greek Independence Day celebration.

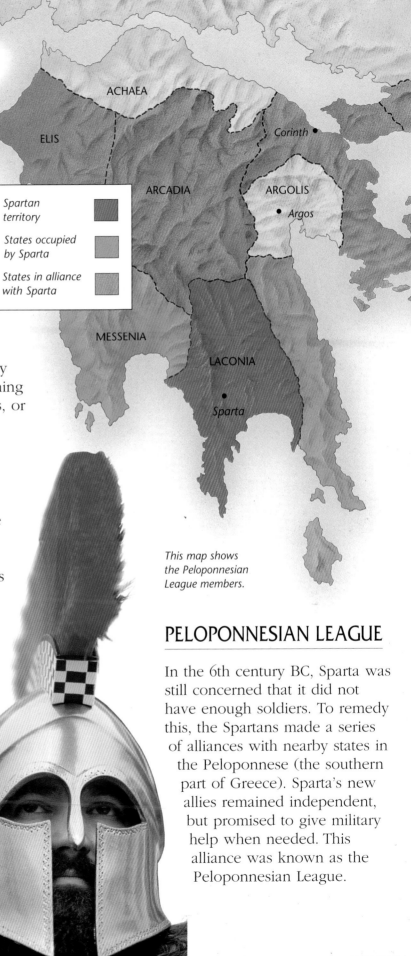

This map shows the Peloponnesian League members.

PELOPONNESIAN LEAGUE

In the 6th century BC, Sparta was still concerned that it did not have enough soldiers. To remedy this, the Spartans made a series of alliances with nearby states in the Peloponnese (the southern part of Greece). Sparta's new allies remained independent, but promised to give military help when needed. This alliance was known as the Peloponnesian League.

THE PELOPONNESIAN WARS

While Athens grew richer and more powerful, the other city-states began to feel threatened. Relations grew worse, especially between Athens and her great rival, Sparta. An atmosphere of suspicion and uneasy peace dragged on until 431BC. Then a war broke out, which tore the Greek world apart, and weakened the city-states beyond repair.

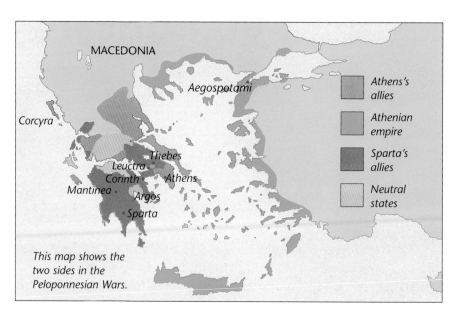

This map shows the two sides in the Peloponnesian Wars.

Map labels: MACEDONIA, Corcyra, Aegospotami, Thebes, Leuctra, Corinth, Mantinea, Athens, Argos, Sparta

Legend:
- Athens's allies
- Athenian empire
- Sparta's allies
- Neutral states

THE LONG WALLS

In 460BC, the Athenians began building vast walls to enclose their city and its sea port at Piraeus. The walls were designed to stop an enemy from cutting Athens off from its navy. The Long Walls, as they were known, effectively turned Athens into a fortress. The Spartans were nervous: they were sure the Athenians must be preparing for war. In 435-433BC, fighting broke out between Corinth and its colony of Corcyra (Corfu).

Sparta and Athens backed opposing sides. Sparta (supported by its allies in the Peloponnesian League) then declared war directly on Athens (and its allies in the Delian League). In 431, the mighty Spartan army marched into the province of Attica, the area immediately around Athens.

This scene shows the Athenians behind the Long Walls defending themselves from a Spartan attack.

THE SIEGE OF ATHENS

While the Athenians could rely on their navy to import food, they could retreat behind the Walls and avoid a land battle. But in 430BC, the city was struck by plague: it lasted four years, killing a quarter of the population, while the Spartans destroyed land all around them. By 421BC, both sides were exhausted and signed a truce.

DEMOCRACY IN PERIL

Life in Athens became very unstable after this. For a while, democracy was even abolished. Desperate for a strong leader, they recalled the traitor Alcibiades from exile. But he failed to solve their problems. Support for the Athenians declined, and some of their allies in the Delian League turned against them.

This coin was issued in Syracuse to commemorate its victory over Athens.

BETRAYAL AND DEFEAT

In 415BC, a politician named Alcibiades persuaded the Athenians to attack Syracuse in Sicily. But, before the attack, he was recalled to Athens to face charges brought against him by his enemies. He fled to Sparta, Syracuse's ally, and betrayed his city. His treachery spelled disaster for Athens: 175 ships were destroyed or captured, and 40,000 men were killed.

SPARTA BUILDS A FLEET

For the Athenians, the final nightmare came when their old enemies, the Persians, joined forces with their rival Sparta. The Persians agreed to fund a fleet of ships: in return, Sparta had to to agree to recognize Persia's claim to Ionia.

The Spartans were now poised to attack at sea as well as on land. In 405BC, they made a surprise attack on the Athenian navy at Aegospotami.

FINAL SURRENDER

Led by their admiral, Lysander, the Spartans won a crushing victory: they captured 170 Athenian ships and executed about 4,000 prisoners. Then they laid siege to Athens itself. Without a fleet of ships, the city was unable to import food. The Athenians were finally starved into surrender in 404BC.

🏺 INTERNET LINKS

For links to websites where you can read a cartoon story about one of the battles and find out more about the wars, go to **www.usborne-quicklinks.com**

THE END OF AN ERA

The conclusion of the Peloponnesian Wars didn't bring peace or unity. Instead it spelled the end of the great days of the city-states, and eventually of the Classical Age. Other squabbles and conflicts followed, in which the Greek cities were far too absorbed to notice a new power rising in the northeast: Macedonia. Within 50 years, the Macedonians would control most of Greece, making it the core of a great empire.

SPARTA IN CONTROL

After the Wars, Athens was ruled by a group of pro-Spartan aristocrats, led by a man named Critias. The Thirty Tyrants, as they were known, made themselves so unpopular that the King of Sparta allowed democracy to be restored in 403BC.

This bronze helmet came from Sparta.

WAR BEGINS AGAIN

Spartan supremacy did not last. Wars broke out again and Sparta lost much of the land it had won. The Persian alliance collapsed too, when the Persians declared war on Sparta over the former Greek colonies in Ionia. Within 10 years, Athens, Thebes, Argos and Corinth were all at war with Sparta. The Spartans were defeated by Thebes at the Battle of Leuctra in 371BC and Thebes took on the role of leading Greek state. Less than 10 years later, the Thebans themselves were beaten by Spartans and Athenians at the Battle of Mantinea in 362BC.

INTERNET LINKS

For a link to a website where you can see a timeline of the major events in the history of ancient Greece, go to **www.usborne-quicklinks.com**

The figure from this painted pot is a Persian archer. Notice how different the costume is from that of a Greek soldier.

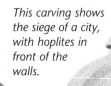

This carving shows the siege of a city, with hoplites in front of the walls.

Grave stele of an Athenian woman, late 5th century BC.

EVERYDAY LIFE

GROWING UP

Greek citizens were taught that it was their patriotic duty to marry and have children. Sons were always preferred, as they would become the next generation of citizens. They would also be able to look after their parents in old age. Daughters could not do this, because they were not allowed to inherit money or property of their own.

This portrait of a woman and her grandchild was carved on a tombstone.

This scene from a water jar shows a nurse handing a baby to its mother.

LIFE OR DEATH

A father could reject a baby if he believed it wasn't his, or if it was disabled. Baby girls were often rejected too. The baby was left to die in an exposed area, such as the top of a mountain. Some babies were abandoned because their parents couldn't afford to keep them. In this case the baby might be adopted and brought up as a slave.

CELEBRATIONS

Seven days after the birth of a baby, friends and family were invited to a party to celebrate the birth. Sacrifices were made to the gods and the guests brought gifts for the child. The door of the house was decorated with garlands - olive branches for a boy and wool for a girl. A special ceremony, called the *Amphidromia*, was held. This was usually when the baby was given its name.

When children reached the age of three, they were no longer regarded as infants. In Athens, this stage of the child's life was celebrated at a spring festival in honour of the god Dionysus, called the *Anthesteria*, or festival of flowers. The children were presented with small jugs during the festivities.

CHILDREN'S TOYS

This odd-shaped feeding bottle (left), bed and potty belonged to a Greek child.

Babies were given rattles and dolls, while older children played with spinning tops, yo-yos and hoops. Richer families even had small-scale furniture, such as stools and cots, made for their children.

EDUCATION

To the ancient Greeks, the purpose of education was to bring up good citizens to take part in running the state. Inevitably, this meant school was limited to boys only. Girls stayed at home, and usually only learned to read and write if their mothers could teach them. School began at the age of seven, but it was not free, so most boys only received a basic education. Richer boys could stay on until the age of 18.

This scene from a Greek pot shows a pupil and his teacher, writing on something that looks like a laptop computer. It's actually a wooden slate coated with wax, which is what children wrote on.

THREE SCHOOLS

There were three types of schools. At the first, the boys were taught reading, writing and arithmetic by a teacher called a *grammatistes*.

At the second school, poetry and music were taught by a teacher called a *kitharistes*. Boys had to learn pieces of poetry by heart, and were taught musical instruments, such as the lyre and the pipes.

At the third school, boys were taught dancing and athletics by a man called a *paidotribes*. Boys took part in competitive games at a training ground called a *gymnasium*.

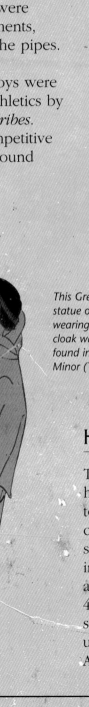

This Greek statue of a boy wearing a short cloak was found in Asia Minor (Turkey).

INTERNET LINKS

For a link to a website with an interactive exhibit about what children's lives were like in ancient Greece, go to **www.usborne-quicklinks.com**

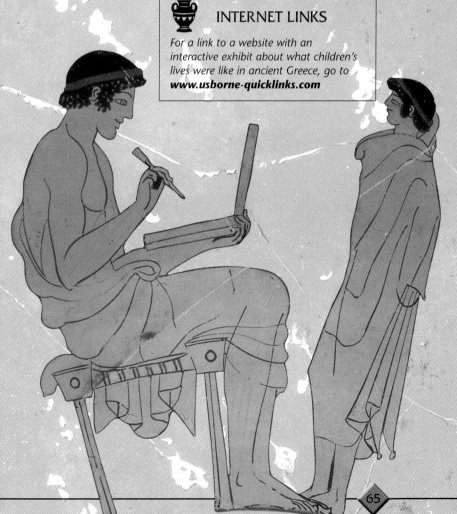

HIGHER EDUCATION

The ancient Greeks did not have universities as we do today, but from the 5th century BC teachers called sophists went from city to city, instructing young men in the art of public speaking. In the 4th century BC, philosophers such as Plato and Aristotle set up schools at *gymnasia* in Athens (see page 121).

WOMEN AND THE HOME

This piece of pottery shows two women deep in conversation. It was made in Asia Minor (Turkey) in about 100BC.

Women in ancient Greece led very sheltered lives - even by the standards of other ancient civilizations. They couldn't take part in politics, or own property. Their lives were always under the control of male relatives: fathers, husbands, brothers, and even sons.

This painting of a wedding procession has been magnified hugely, as it was painted on a tiny pottery box. A bride is being driven to her new home in a chariot.

MARRIAGE

A girl usually married when she was only about 15 years old, but her husband could be much older than she was. The philosopher Plato suggested that 30-35 was the best age for a man to marry. The husband was chosen by the girl's father, who provided her dowry. This was a gift of money and goods, which was looked after by the husband.

CHILDHOOD ENDS

The day before the wedding, the bride sacrificed her toys to the goddess Artemis, to symbolize the end of her childhood. Then she bathed in water from a sacred spring, carried to the bath in a special vase called a *loutrophoros*. These vases were often decorated with scenes of the wedding ceremony.

THE WEDDING DAY

On the day, both families made sacrifices to the gods and held feasts in separate houses. Then, in the evening, the groom went to his bride's home. This was often the first time that they had met.

The couple then made their way back to the groom's house. If they were rich, they were driven by chariot, led by torch-bearers and musicians. Poorer people had to make do with a simple cart.

The bride was carried over the threshold, as a symbol that she was joining the religious life of the new family. The family scattered fruits and nuts over them for luck.

INTERNET LINKS

For links to websites where you can find out more about the lives of women in ancient Greece, go to **www.usborne-quicklinks.com**

TIED TO THE HOME?

In Athens, for rich married women at least, there was very little life outside the home. They were permitted to visit female friends, or to invite them to dinner, but these were women-only affairs. They had very few other opportunities to leave the house.

Much of a woman's day was taken up with making cloth. This painting shows a woman spinning.

A WOMAN'S ROLE

At home, a woman played a vital role. She managed the finances, food, housework, spinning and weaving, and cared for the children and for anyone else in the family if they fell ill.

This Greek pottery figure shows a woman cooking.

One compensation for women from poorer familes was that they could get out more. They had to go shopping and collect water from the wells, which gave them more of a chance to see life outside the confines of their home. Some even had jobs as innkeepers.

DIVORCE

A wife was expected to be devoted to her husband. If he suspected her of being unfaithful, he could divorce her and keep her dowry - and the children as well.

A DIFFERENT LIFE

Not all girls were brought up to be good, obedient wives. Some, known as *hetairai*, became companions to rich men. They lived in great comfort and could even attend men's dinner parties.

GREEK HOUSES

Very few Greek houses have been excavated, because they were built of mud brick, which does not last. But we have a good idea of what they were like from the ones that have been found, and because the design of houses in the Mediterranean has changed so little over the centuries.

A COURTYARD HOUSE

A typical house was built around a courtyard, with doors to each room, and a few small windows in the outside walls. The walls were made of mud brick, on stone foundations, with wooden doors and window shutters. There were stone slabs on the floors of the courtyard, and mosaics or stone slabs on the floors downstairs on the inside. The roof was covered with clay tiles.

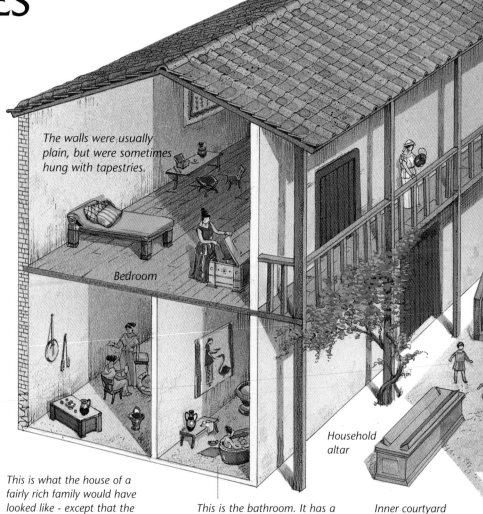

The walls were usually plain, but were sometimes hung with tapestries.

Bedroom

This is what the house of a fairly rich family would have looked like - except that the front walls have been taken away so you can see inside.

This is the bathroom. It has a bathtub of baked clay, with a drain which leads outside.

Household altar

Inner courtyard

SEPARATE LIVES

The men and women in a wealthy Greek household lived very separate lives, in separate parts of the house.

Floors were sometimes decorated with patterns like this, called mosaics, made from tiny pieces of stone.

Although most houses had a single floor, some had two. The men ate and entertained in a downstairs room called the *andron*. The kitchen and bathroom were also downstairs, as well as a special room, dedicated to Hestia, goddess of the hearth, which was used for family gatherings.

This baked clay, or terracotta, statue is of a woman making bread.

FURNITURE

Most houses were very simply furnished, with plain wooden tables, chairs and beds. In richer households, the furniture might be decorated with elaborate patterns, with ivory, gold or silver inlaid into the wood.

The women's room, called the gynaeceum

This wall has been removed, so you can see inside the kitchen.

The dining room, or andron

The walls of the house were made of mud bricks, sometimes reinforced with wooden beams.

In winter, portable metal stoves which burned charcoal were used to heat the rooms.

Most people sat on stools, like this one, except the head of a rich household who had an armchair called a thronos (right).

Tables were usually low, so that they could be pushed under couches when not in use. They were either round, oval or rectangular, with three legs or a single support.

Wooden couches and beds were strung with cords or leather thongs, with mattresses, pillows and covers on top.

Clothes and bedding were stored in wooden chests, while smaller items were kept in boxes and baskets.

UPSTAIRS ROOMS

In a house like the one here, the family bedrooms, the servants' quarters, and the women's rooms, known as the *gynaeceum*, were all upstairs. Women from the richer families led very sheltered lives. They spent most of their time confined to their rooms, organizing the household, spinning, weaving, and talking to other women friends.

LIGHTING

Greek houses were lit by small oil-burning lamps, made of pottery, bronze or even silver. Oil was poured into the round body of the lamp. Then you lit a wick (a piece of string coated with wax), which was sticking out of the spout.

Spout

Oil-burning lamp

CLOTHES AND FASHION

Greek clothes were extremely simple in design. Men wore tunics and women wore a robe called a *chiton*. Both were made from one or two rectangular pieces of cloth, sewn up the sides and fastened at the shoulders with pins and brooches.

MEN'S CLOTHES

Tunics were normally knee-length for young men, and ankle-length for older men. They were often worn with a belt and hitched up over it to keep them in place. When the weather was particularly hot, craftsmen and slaves often wore nothing more than a loincloth tied around the waist, to keep them cool.

This is the sort of plain, short tunic many men would have worn.

In cold weather, people sometimes wore cloaks as well. A long one was called a *himation*, a short one was a *chlamys*. Out in the sun, people often wore shady, wide-brimmed hats.

A chlamys was usually worn by soldiers, or by younger men for hunting or riding.

WOMEN'S CLOTHES

There were two styles of chiton: Doric and Ionic. The Doric chiton was a single piece of cloth, folded over at the top and wrapped loosely around the body, with a belt, and brooches at the shoulders to make armholes.

The Ionic chiton was made from two pieces of cloth, stitched up the sides and fastened along the shoulders and arms with brooches.

This woman is wearing an Ionic chiton. This style may have come from the Greek colony of Ionia.

This woman is wearing a shawl called a himation, over an Ionic chiton. A himation could be a thin, light scarf, or a thick, heavy cloak for cold weather or journeys.

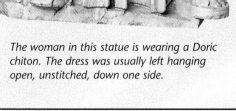

The woman in this statue is wearing a Doric chiton. The dress was usually left hanging open, unstitched, down one side.

CHANGING FASHIONS

These women weaving on a loom, wearing highly patterned dresses, were painted on an Archaic Period vase.

Most people's clothes were made of plain wool or linen, although richer people could afford to dye or decorate them. Bright, patterned fabrics were popular in the Archaic Period. Later, clothes were often of one shade, sometimes with a patterned border.

 INTERNET LINKS

For links to websites where you can see clothing and ornaments worn by the ancient Greeks, go to
www.usborne-quicklinks.com

BEAUTY REGIME

Rich women bathed every day and rubbed themselves with perfumed oils. Powdered chalk was used to make their skin look fashionably pale. They also used a red powder on their cheeks and a darker one for emphasizing their eyebrows.

This Greek pottery model shows a woman in a bathtub. It is only big enough for sitting up in.

HAIRSTYLES

Fashion in hairstyles changed over the centuries. As time went on, men's hair and beards grew shorter and tidier, and women's hairstyles became higher and more elaborately styled.

Simple styles from the Archaic Period

In Classical times, women put up their hair with ribbons, hairnets, scarves or gold bands. Men's beards were tidier.

In the Hellenistic Period, men shaved off their beards and women styled their hair with waves and curls.

SHOES

These Greek scent bottles, shaped like feet, show us what their sandals looked like.

Most Greeks went barefoot for much of the time, or wore strappy leather sandals. But they did have other styles of shoes, such as calf-length boots for horsemen.

Mirror glass had not been invented in ancient times, so hand mirrors like this one were made of highly polished bronze.

FARMING AND FOOD

Most people in ancient Greece lived by farming, although the land wasn't always easy to cultivate. There was good farmland by the coast and in the valleys. But the rest of the country was rugged, rocky and mountainous - suitable only for grazing mountain sheep and goats.

A TYPICAL FARM

Ancient Greek farms were usually fairly small and only produced enough food to feed one family, with a little extra to sell at the local market. They were worked by the owner, his family, and a few workers or slaves. Citizens from the towns often owned farms too, and paid a manager to look after them.

WHEAT AND BARLEY

Wheat and barley were the most important crops. They were used to make bread and porridge, which formed the major part of the diet - at least for poorer people. The grain was sown in October and harvested in April or May. After this, the field was left fallow (unplanted) for a time, so that the soil could regain its goodness.

This is a modern photograph of a typical Greek landscape. It still looks much as it would have in ancient times.

OLIVES AND GRAPES

Olives and grapes were among the most important crops. Most olives were crushed in a press to make oil, which the ancient Greeks relied on for a great many things: medicines, cosmetics and lighting, as well as cooking. Grapes were grown for eating, or pressed to be made into wine.

This Greek vase shows people picking olives.

FARM ANIMALS

Farmers kept pigs and poultry for their meat, and sheep and goats for their milk and hides too. Cows were not common. Horses were bred in the region of Thessaly, where there was a lot of good pasture. Oxen and mules were used as working animals on farms. The oxen pulled heavy equipment and mules pulled carts and carried loads.

 INTERNET LINKS

For links to websites where you can find ancient Greek food facts, pictures and recipes, go to
www.usborne-quicklinks.com

WHAT PEOPLE ATE

The ancient Greeks ate many of the same sorts of things that we do. The main difference was that most people ate more porridge and bread than anything else. Greek bread was usually made from barley, as it was cheaper than wheat.

This is a hunter and his dog, from a Greek vase painting.

The Greeks also ate fish, cheese, vegetables and fruit, but relatively little meat - apart from wild animals that they could hunt, such as hares, deer and boars. Coriander, sesame and honey were often used to add taste, but not sugar - because they didn't have any.

THE MARKETPLACE

At the heart of every Greek city was a main square, or marketplace, called an *agora*. It was the focus for business life and a hub of local gossip - a meeting place, where people gathered to shop, do business, catch up on the latest news and chat with their friends.

BUYING AND SELLING

Storekeepers often sold their goods in open rooms, with a counter across the front, behind a row of columns in a building in the *agora* called a *stoa*. Local farmers also set up temporary stalls in the middle of the square. Meat and fish were often displayed on marble slabs, which kept the food cool in the hot sun.

This is an agora in a typical Greek city. Notice the acropolis above the main square.

Friends could meet in the shade under the columns of the stoa.

The men usually did the shopping. Most women only went out accompanied by their male relatives.

A statue of a local god, a politican or an athlete often stood in the main square.

Altar for sacrifices to the gods

Workers for hire

Slaves being sold on a platform called a kykloi

Local farmers and craftsmen selling goods such as pots, olives, and vegetables

WEIGHTS AND MEASURES

Traders in the *agora* were controlled by different officials. In Athens, ten *metronomoi* were chosen annually to check weights and measures, to ensure that the customers were not cheated with short measures. Officials called *agoranomoi* checked the quality of the goods, while *sitophylakes* were specifically in charge of keeping an eye on the grain trade.

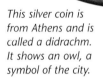

The coin on the left is an electrum coin from Cyzicus, a Greek colony in Ionia. It shows the god Poseidon with a fish.

This silver coin is from Athens and is called a didrachm. It shows an owl, a symbol of the city.

THE FIRST BANKS

By the 6th century BC, each city was issuing its own coins, which became a sign of its independence. People who wanted to do business in another city had to change their money with a moneychanger. These people charged a fee, and often made such a profit that they lent money too.

A moneychanger sometimes helped people who had money to spare. He would find a suitable venture for them to invest in, and pay them interest from the profits.

These Hellenistic Period gold coins show Ptolemy I of Egypt (left) and Alexander the Great in a chariot drawn by elephants.

THE FIRST COINS

Coins were probably invented at the end of the 7th century BC in Lydia, a kingdom in Asia Minor. They were made of electrum (a mixture of gold and silver). The idea spread to the Greek colonies in Ionia and then to mainland Greece. Sparta was the only state that didn't adopt coins until later, in the 4th century BC.

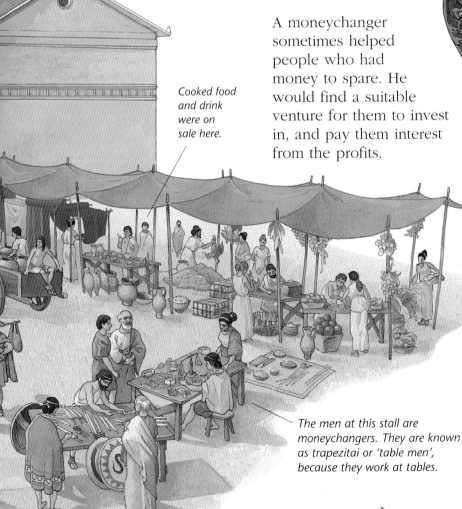

Cooked food and drink were on sale here.

The men at this stall are moneychangers. They are known as trapezitai or 'table men', because they work at tables.

INTERNET LINKS

For links to websites where you can watch a movie about Greek coins and tour a Greek agora, go to **www.usborne-quicklinks.com**

ARCHITECTURE

The architects of Classical Greece built according to strict mathematical rules, carefully calculating proportions - such as the height and number of columns - to give their buildings a feeling of balance, simplicity and elegance. Their results were so successful that they have been seen as a model for architecture ever since.

THE BASIC DESIGN

The design of most temples and other public buildings in ancient Greece was based on a series of vertical columns, with a horizontal beam across them. This idea may have developed from much earlier times, when tree trunks would have been used to support a roof. There were two main styles, or orders, of ancient Greek architecture. They are known as Doric and Ionic.

Doric capital

Ionic capital

THE DORIC STYLE

The Doric style was the most popular on the Greek mainland. The design was simple, with thick, powerful columns. The tops of the columns, or capitals, were undecorated.

Cornice

A reconstruction of the facade (front) of a Doric temple

The pediment (the triangular part) was carved with sculptures and painted.

Plain capital

Frieze carved with panels of sculpture, called metopes

The part above the columns, and below the pediment, is called the entablature.

The architrave (lowest part of the entablature)

INTERNET LINKS

For links to websites where you can find out more about Greek architecture and test yourself with an online game, go to **www.usborne-quicklinks.com**

This photograph shows what is left today of the Temple of Poseidon, in Paestum, Italy, which was built in the Doric style.

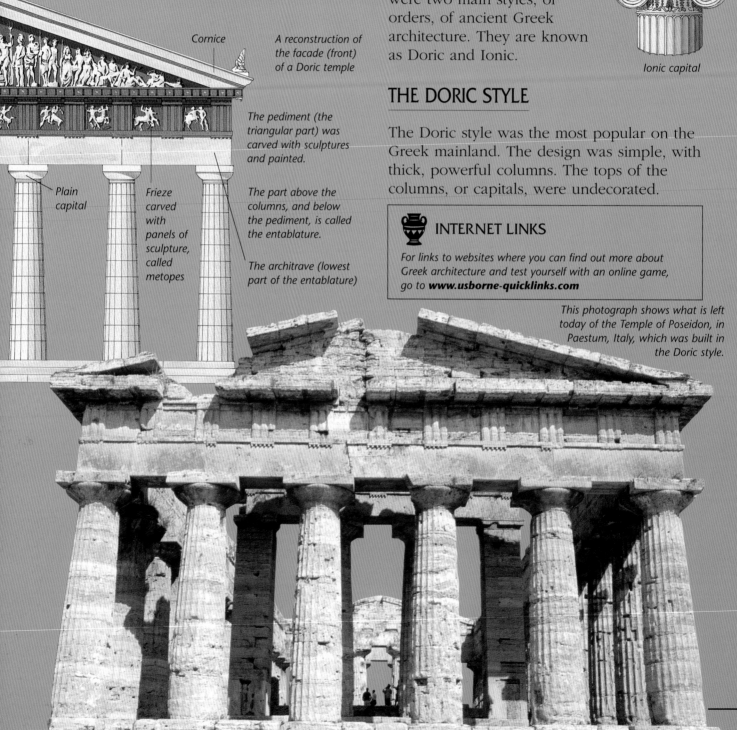

THE IONIC STYLE

The Ionic style was a more elegant, decorated style than the Doric, using slender columns with bases and decorated capitals with spiral curls known as volutes. It was particularly popular in the eastern colonies of Asia Minor and on the Aegean islands.

These are the ruins of the Erectheum temple, built in the Ionic style, which is on the Acropolis in Athens. The pediment and roof have worn away with time and pollution.

These are caryatids, female statues used as columns

Pediment (triangular space)

The frieze went all the way around the building in a continuous band.

Ionic capitals were decorated with a curl on each side, called a volute.

Stepped base

Above is a reconstruction of the front of a typical Ionic temple, with its parts labelled.

OTHER STYLES

The Aeolic capital was an early form of Ionic capital, found at Smyrna in Asia Minor (Turkey) and on the island of Lesbos. It dates back to the 6th century BC.

Aeolic capital

The Corinthian capital was a later, more ornate style, decorated with a leafy pattern. Although the Greeks rarely used it, it became very popular later with the Romans.

Corinthian capital

A LASTING INFLUENCE

Ancient Greek architecture has had a lasting influence on the architecture of the world. It impressed the Romans so much that they copied and adapted it, but it has also inspired countless other imitations over the centuries, in many different countries. Buildings in the Classical Greek style of architecture are often known as Neoclassical.

The 19th-century Capitol building, in Washington D.C., has Corinthian capitals and a facade like a Greek temple.

BUILDING

The Greek city-states commissioned architects and sculptors to construct magnificent public buildings and monuments. Most of them were made of marble or limestone, with wooden beams to support the roof, which was covered with tiles made of marble or terracotta (a type of baked clay). The insides were decorated with sculptures and the outsides with panels of carved stone, called reliefs.

Mythological beasts, like this winged monster called a griffin, were among the things the Greeks carved on temple walls.

This Greek head, shaped like a lion, would have decorated the side of a temple. There are still traces of paint attached to the stone.

CARVING IN MARBLE

Greek sculptors worked in marble because it is hard enough to last and fine enough for carving detail.

Blocks of stone were dug out of a quarry and carved into a rough shape at the site, before being transported to the sculptor's workshop. Most statues we see today are bare stone, but they were originally brightly painted. It's just that all the paint has long since worn off.

Sometimes bright glass, stone or metal was used for eyes, and details such as jewels or weapons were made of bronze.

This sculpture of Nike, goddess of victory, came from the temple of Apollo at Delphi.

BUILDING A TEMPLE

Temples were the most important buildings in ancient Greece. They were the focus both for religious feeling and local pride. Here you can see how the Greeks constructed a temple, without the help of cranes or cement.

Workmen cut the stone into cylindrical pieces for the columns, leaving stone handles on the sides so they could be lifted with ropes. The handles were chipped off later.

Metal rods known as dowels joined each block to the one above and below.

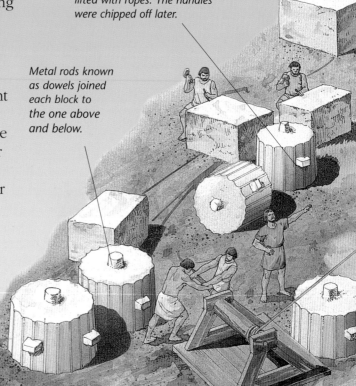

Workmen climbed up on wooden ladders and scaffolding.

Ropes and pulleys were used to lift the blocks of stone and hoist them into position, one on top of the other. Then they were eased into place with levers.

Carts like this one carried large blocks of stone from the quarry to the building site.

Blocks of stone were joined with pieces of metal called cramps.

SCULPTURE

The ancient Greeks carved some of the finest sculptures ever made. They set a standard for the portrayal of the human body that has been imitated and admired ever since. Many of the original sculptures were lost, or carried off by invaders after the end of the Classical era. But we know what many of them looked like, because the Romans made thousands of copies that still survive.

The features on this Archaic Period limestone head look quite Eastern.

To decorate their temples, the Greeks carved figures and mythological scenes, known as reliefs, on flat slabs of stone. This one shows the gods Poseidon and Apollo and the goddesses Artemis and Athene.

ARCHAIC PERIOD c.800-480BC

Early sculptures were carved in a simple, formal style, copied from Egyptian art. Figures were shown standing stiffly, with the left leg forward and the arms at the side. The face was carved with a half-smile. There were two main types: a male nude, called a *kouros*, and a clothed female, called a *kore*.

Later sculptors began carving figures in more relaxed poses, to make them look realistic.

A statue of an Egyptian queen

The figure of a young woman, or kore, on the left is from Greece, c.650BC. If you compare it with the figure above, you may notice her hairstyle looks Egyptian.

 INTERNET LINKS

For links to websites where you can see lots of Greek sculptures and explore a timeline, go to **www.usborne-quicklinks.com**

CLASSICAL PERIOD c.480-323BC

This marble discus thrower is a Roman copy of a bronze statue of c.450BC, by a well-known Greek sculptor named Myron.

The sculptors of the Classical period perfected the art of portraying the human body in a realistic, natural-looking way.

Their figures were noted for their beauty and serenity. There was a growing interest in portraying the female body. Many sculptors became skilled at showing facial expressions and emotions, and produced recognizable portraits of famous people. To demonstrate their skill, figures were often shown in active poses, such as taking part in sports.

This marble head of the goddess Aphrodite is one of the most famous works of a sculptor named Praxiteles.

The reputation of Athenian artists soon spread abroad, and their work was exported all around the Mediterranean. Factories were set up near marble quarries, to try to meet the demand.

This headless statue of the goddess of victory, the Victory of Samothrace, was carved c.190BC to commemorate a victory at sea.

It was originally part of a larger sculpture, which had the goddess landing on a ship's prow - which explains her outstretched wings and swirling clothes.

HELLENISTIC PERIOD c.323-100BC

In the Hellenistic Period, sculptors began to portray a much wider range of characters. Where Classical artists had concentrated on gods and famous men, children, foreigners and old people were now possible subjects. Sculptures from this time could be very dramatic too. Instead of just calm, serene poses, Hellenistic sculptors tackled subjects such as old age, pain and even death.

POTTERY

Greek pots came in many different shapes. Here are the most common styles.

Kylix

Skyphos

Kantharos

The first three pots shown here were drinking cups used at parties.

Kraters were large two-handled pots for mixing wine with water. The two main types were calyx kraters and volute kraters (with spiral handles).

Calyx krater

Voluté krater

The wine and water mixture was then poured into a jug known as an oinochoe. It was then poured into cups to drink.

Oinochoe

The ancient Greeks are famous for their painted pottery, often known as 'vase painting'. The amazingly detailed and varied scenes they painted on their pottery have given us an enormous amount of information about their daily lives and their myths and legends.

GEOMETRIC STYLE

From about 1000-700BC, during the Dark Ages, Greek pots were decorated with zigzag and geometric patterns. Later in this period, figures of animals and people began to be added to the designs, painted in between the bands of geometric decoration.

This Dark Age pot is painted with intricate geometric patterns.

ORIENTAL STYLE

From about 720 to 550BC, contacts with foreigners, such as the Egyptians, led to what is called the "Orientalizing" style. Many designs included motifs, such as lotuses, palms and mythical monsters, that

This animal-headed jug dates back to about 600BC.

were common in Egyptian art. Later in the period, scenes from Greek mythology and daily life started to appear on pots. The figures were also more detailed and realistic than they had been earlier.

A kylix painted by a well-known Athenian artist named Exekias

ATHENIAN POTTERY

Some of the most detailed and sophisticated vase painting was produced in Athens between 550-300BC. Artists decorated pots with scenes from daily life, as well as from Greek mythology.

The earliest Athenian pottery, from about 550BC, is known as black-figure ware, because black figures were shown on a red background. From about 530BC, they also made red-figure ware: red figures on a black background. A few pots were painted on white backgrounds too.

 INTERNET LINKS

For links to websites where you can see lots of Greek pots, try a quiz and watch a video of how they were made, go to
www.usborne-quicklinks.com

MAKING BLACK- AND RED-FIGURE WARE

Athenian potters used a clay that turned red when fired. The areas of the pot that were to be black were filled in with a black paint made from clay, ash and water. Red-figure pots were painted black, with the figures left bare, or cut into the surface, so that they showed through in red after the clay was fired. Touches of white and dark red paint were used for fine details.

During the firing process, the openings to the kiln were shut. This cut off the oxygen supply, turning the pot black. The temperature was left to drop and the air vents were reopened - the painted areas stayed black, and the rest turned red.

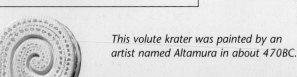

This volute krater was painted by an artist named Altamura in about 470BC.

An aryballos and alabastron were delicate flasks for perfumed oils and ointments.

Aryballos

Alabastron

This is a loutrophoros, a large vase with a long neck, used for carrying water for a bride's ceremonial bath.

Loutrophoros

This flat round box, known as a pyxis, was used for storing medicines.

Pyxis

This is an amphora, a two-handled jar used to store wine, oil and other liquids.

Amphora

A hydria was a jar for carrying water from fountains. Two handles were used to lift it, while a third, on the neck, was used for pouring.

Hydria

METALWORK

Bronze was the main metal used by the Greeks for their weapons and tools from Mycenaean times on. Iron was introduced in the Dark Ages. Gold and silver were used too, but only for more precious items.

METALSMITHS

Most metalsmiths worked in small workshops at home, but in Athens they had their own quarter near the temple of Hephaestos, the patron god of metalsmiths.

The picture on this pot shows a metalsmith at work on a helmet.

BRONZE

Bronze is a valuable metal, made by mixing a small amount of tin with copper. Many of the larger statues that were made of bronze were melted down for reuse, so very few still exist today. Two larger than life-size statues that have survived were fished out of the sea off southern Italy in 1972. They date back to 450BC and are known as the Riace warriors.

This is the head of one of the Riace warriors. The lips were made of copper, and the eyelashes and teeth of silver.

WORKING BRONZE

HAMMERING
The earliest bronze statues were made from flat sheets of bronze which were hammered out and riveted over a wooden core, sometimes called a shape.

CASTING
Later, small statues were made of solid metal, cast inside a shape. Larger statues were made in several sections, then joined together afterwards.

LOST WAX
Some statues were made by a method called lost wax.

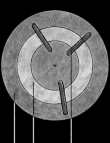

1. The statue was shaped in wax around a clay core.

2. The model was covered with more clay and heated. The wax melted and ran out, leaving a gap between the two layers of clay.

3. Molten bronze was poured into the gap. When it cooled and set, the clay shape was removed, revealing the statue.

Pins hold core in place.

Wax shaped around clay core

Outer clay shape

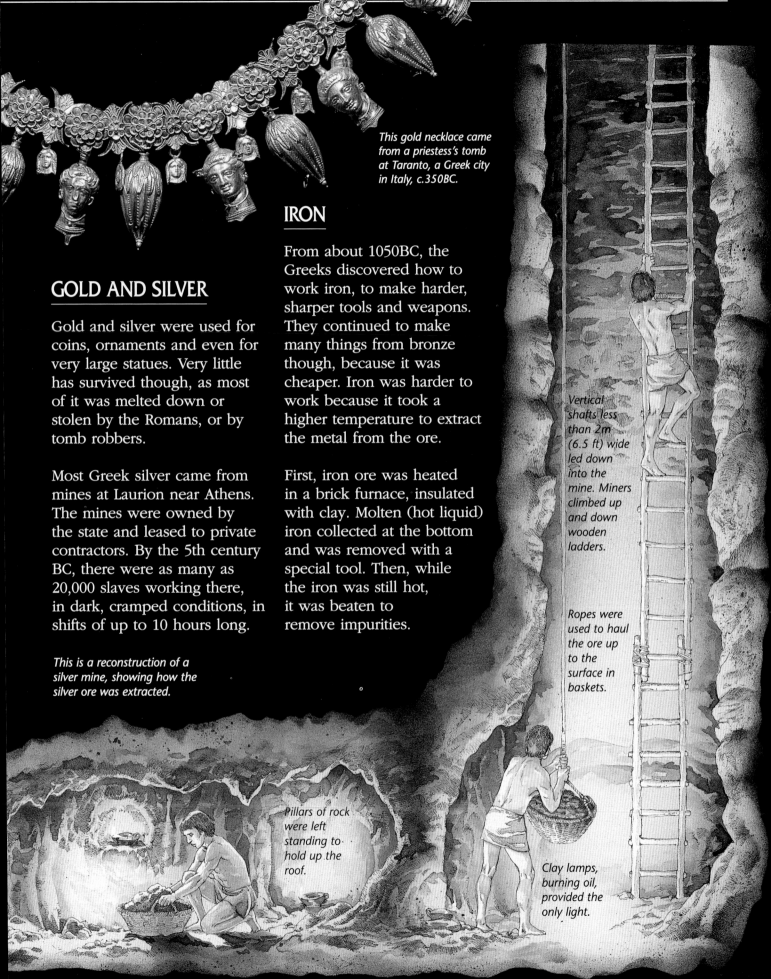

This gold necklace came from a priestess's tomb at Taranto, a Greek city in Italy, c.350BC.

GOLD AND SILVER

Gold and silver were used for coins, ornaments and even for very large statues. Very little has survived though, as most of it was melted down or stolen by the Romans, or by tomb robbers.

Most Greek silver came from mines at Laurion near Athens. The mines were owned by the state and leased to private contractors. By the 5th century BC, there were as many as 20,000 slaves working there, in dark, cramped conditions, in shifts of up to 10 hours long.

This is a reconstruction of a silver mine, showing how the silver ore was extracted.

IRON

From about 1050BC, the Greeks discovered how to work iron, to make harder, sharper tools and weapons. They continued to make many things from bronze though, because it was cheaper. Iron was harder to work because it took a higher temperature to extract the metal from the ore.

First, iron ore was heated in a brick furnace, insulated with clay. Molten (hot liquid) iron collected at the bottom and was removed with a special tool. Then, while the iron was still hot, it was beaten to remove impurities.

Vertical shafts less than 2m (6.5 ft) wide led down into the mine. Miners climbed up and down wooden ladders.

Ropes were used to haul the ore up to the surface in baskets.

Pillars of rock were left standing to hold up the roof.

Clay lamps, burning oil, provided the only light.

TRAVEL BY LAND AND SEA

The Greek interior is rugged and mountainous. Some remote areas can be perilous and difficult to pass in winter, even now, but in ancient times it was far worse, as there were hardly any roads. With a coastline full of natural ports and inlets, it was much easier to travel by sea - although it was laden with all kinds of dangers nevertheless, either from the weather and natural difficulties, or from other sea voyagers.

INTERNET LINKS

For links to websites where you can investigate a Greek shipwreck and read the adventures of Odysseus and Jason, go to **www.usborne-quicklinks.com**

PIRATES, STORMS AND SHIPWRECKS

People who didn't have their own ship could pay merchant seamen to take them, but all sea journeys were fairly risky. Once the ship had set sail, dishonest sailors might rob their passengers, or the ship might be attacked by pirates. Piracy was a real and constant fear, until the 5th century BC, when the Athenian navy began to patrol the Aegean and reduced the number of attacks. Another potential danger was that of being sunk in a storm. Marine archaeologists have explored the remains of several ancient wrecks off the Greek coast.

THE KYRENIA SHIP

One merchant ship, discovered in the waters off Kyrenia in Cyprus in 1967, was raised to the surface and restored. Known as the Kyrenia ship, it originally sank around 300BC.

This is a reconstruction of the Kyrenia ship. The side of the ship has been cut away so you can see the cargo.

The mast was made of spruce wood and the hull of pine. This timber had to be imported from the woods of Thrace or Macedonia.

The large, square sail was made of linen.

The ropes were made of flax or hemp.

Two large oars at the back to steer the ship

MAPPING THE WORLD

The Greeks were skilled at navigating and making maps. In the 6th century BC, a man named Thales who was from Miletus went to Egypt to study mathematics and astronomy He brought his specialist knowledge back to Greece and became the first person there to find a method of measuring the distance of a ship from the sea shore.

Another Greek scholar, named Anaximander, became the first to draw a map of the world, although it does not survive today for us to check its accuracy.

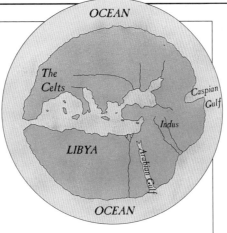

This 6th century BC map by Hecataeus shows that Greek knowledge of the world extended as far as North Africa, Western Europe and Asia Minor.

This 5th century BC map by Herodotus shows that, by then, knowledge of Asia had increased and the Greeks knew the Caspian Sea was bordered by land.

There are many images of sea creatures in Greek art and legend. This bronze figure is of a boy riding a dolphin.

TRAVEL OVERLAND

Travel overland was painfully slow, as most people had no choice but to walk everywhere. Donkeys were used to carry goods, but only the rich could afford to ride horses. Carts could be used, but only when the roads were good enough for them - which was not often. Then there was the added danger of attacks by bandits and wars between states, which often meant people were forced to make detours lasting many days, just to travel in safety.

This cart is based on a vase painting dated around 540BC. Greek carts had either four or two wheels.

FEASTING AND FUN

For the ancient Greeks, dinner was the most important meal of the day, and it was always eaten late in the evening. For people who could afford it, it was also an opportunity to entertain friends.

This Greek plate shows the sort of fish that would have been eaten at dinner parties.

A GREEK DINNER PARTY

Greek dinner parties were generally all male-affairs. Women were forbidden to join in, except at family gatherings, although male guests could bring female companions, called *hetairai*.

Guests were met at the front door of the house by slaves, who washed their hands and feet, and put garlands of leaves or flowers on their heads. Then they were led into the dining room, where they reclined on couches.

THE FOOD

The food was served by slaves from small tables. There were no forks, so the guests used their fingers, or pieces of bread, to scoop it up. However, table manners were imporant, and they were sometimes written down to help people. Each course had several dishes to choose from. There was probably a fish dish, followed by a meat course, such as mutton, beef, pork or small birds. The meal finished with fruit, such as figs, grapes, pears and apples, and sweet cakes made of honey and nuts.

Grapes, both eaten and drunk as wine, featured on the menu at Greek dinners.

WINE AND DISCUSSION

The most stimulating part of a dinner party was called a *symposium*. This was when the food was cleared away and the guests concentrated on serious conversation. The discussions usually covered weighty topics, such as politics, philosophy or morals. They drank wine, which was mixed with water in a large vase called a krater and then ladled into cups. Three offerings of wine, known as libations, were made to the gods before the guests themselves began drinking.

A kithara, an elaborate stringed instrument rather like a lyre, and a timpanon, an early tambourine

MUSIC, POETRY AND DANCING

The symposium was usually a solemn occasion, but at some dinner parties this part of the evening was much more relaxed. Guests sometimes played musical instruments, sang songs, recited poems or told jokes. At some parties, professional dancers, musicians and acrobats were hired to amuse the guests.

This scene showing after-dinner activities comes from a 5th century BC drinking cup. One musician is playing the double pipes, an instrument seen in many Greek paintings.

GAMES

Although most Greeks worked very hard, they seem to have had time to play games. Several board games, similar to chess, were popular. Apart from the great athletic competitions (see page 92), the Greeks also played more informal sports, including a type of hockey, using a ball and sticks.

Some people also enjoyed cruel sports, such as cat or dog fights. Games such as dice, or knuckle-bones, in which small animal bones were thrown like dice, were played at home or in special gaming houses.

These pottery figures show two women playing a game called knuckle-bones.

INTERNET LINKS

For links where you can watch a movie about Greek parties and listen to a poem, go to ***www.usborne-quicklinks.com***

PLAYS AND PLAYERS

The Western idea of drama is deeply rooted in ancient Greece. In Europe, the very first plays probably developed from songs and dances, performed as part of a Greek religious festival held for Dionysus, the god of wine.

THE DIONYSIA

In Athens, the early religious festival grew into a much larger dramatic festival, the Dionysia, held for five days each spring. Processions and sacrifices were followed by drama competitions. Everyone was allowed to stop work so that they could attend. Aspiring writers submitted their plays to the archon, who chose which ones would be performed.

THE EARLY PLAYS

The early festivals consisted of a group of men, known as the chorus, dancing and singing. Later, an actor was brought in to exchange dialogue with the leader of the chorus. As more actors were introduced, the role of the chorus dwindled, and the dialogue between the actors became the most important part of the play. In this way the modern idea of a play was born.

Comedies, like the one shown here which comes from a Greek pot, contained a lot of clowning around and rude jokes.

TRAGEDIES AND COMEDIES

Greek plays soon evolved into two distinct types: tragedies and comedies. Tragedies were usually about heroes of Greek myths and dealt with moral choices, passions and conflict, and often had unhappy endings. Comedies were about ordinary people, and often mocked leading politicians and personalities of the day.

INTERNET LINKS

For a link to a website where you can go on a trip to watch plays in ancient Greece, go to **www.usborne-quicklinks.com**

This is a chorus member dressed as a bird.

THE STAGE

In Athens, the first plays were performed in the agora - but, as the festival grew bigger, a huge open-air auditorium was built near the Acropolis. This idea was soon copied all over Greece, and some venues could hold over 18,000 spectators.

This picture shows a play being performed in a large open-air auditorium.

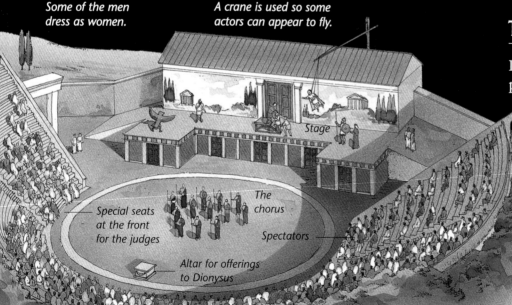

Some of the men dress as women.

A crane is used so some actors can appear to fly.

Stage

Special seats at the front for the judges

The chorus

Spectators

Altar for offerings to Dionysus

IDENTITY MASKS

Greek theatres were cleverly designed so that everyone could hear well, but the auditorium was so large that people sitting at the back were too far from the stage to see clearly. So the actors, who were always men, wore masks to show who they were - man or woman, young or old - and what mood they were in. Some masks were reversible: they had calm expressions on one side and angry ones on the other, so the actor could change moods with a twist of his hand.

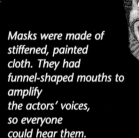

Masks were made of stiffened, painted cloth. They had funnel-shaped mouths to amplify the actors' voices, so everyone could hear them.

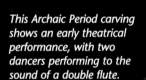

This Archaic Period carving shows an early theatrical performance, with two dancers performing to the sound of a double flute.

COSTUMES

The actors wore special costumes - wigs, thick padded tunics and shoes with thick soles - to make them look larger and taller. Bright clothes meant they were playing happy characters, and dark clothes were for tragic roles. In comedies, the chorus also wore special outfits and sometimes dressed up as birds and other animals.

These characters are from a modern production of the Oresteia, a play by Aeschylus, who is regarded as the founder of Greek tragedy.

THE GAMES

Athletic competitions were held in ancient Greece as part of a religious ceremony for a god or goddess. They were enormously popular and everyone was encouraged to take part. Most of the competitions were local affairs, but some attracted athletes and spectators from all over the Greek world.

This athlete was painted on a Greek pot. None of the contestants wore any clothes.

THE OLYMPIC GAMES

The Olympic Games - the ancestor of the modern Games - was the most famous of all the games. It lasted five days, and was held every four years at Olympia, as part of a festival for the god Zeus.

Wars were brought to a standstill, just so that people could travel to the Games in safety, and magnificent temples and stadiums were built for the occasion. Often, as many as 50,000 people came, some from as far away as Spain and Egypt.

THE MAIN EVENTS

One of the most challenging events in the Games was designed to find the best all-round athlete. This was the *pentathlon*, from the Greek words *pente* (five) and *athlon* (contest). There were five events: discus and javelin-throwing, running, jumping and wrestling.

Running was the oldest event and opened the first day of the Games. There were three main races: the *stade* (one length of the track), *diaulos* (two lengths), and the *dolichos* (20 or 24 lengths). The track was about 192m (640ft) long.

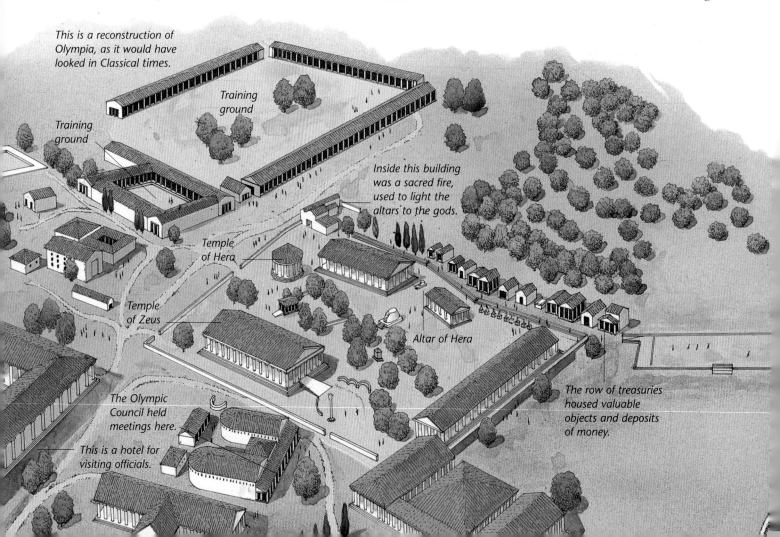

This is a reconstruction of Olympia, as it would have looked in Classical times.

Training ground

Training ground

Inside this building was a sacred fire, used to light the altars to the gods.

Temple of Hera

Temple of Zeus

Altar of Hera

The row of treasuries housed valuable objects and deposits of money.

The Olympic Council held meetings here.

This is a hotel for visiting officials.

HORSE AND CHARIOT RACING

Horse races were run over a distance of about 1200m (nearly a mile). In one race, the rider ran part of the way beside his horse. Jockeys rode bareback (without saddles) and accidents were common.

Chariot racing was probably the most popular event. Chariots, pulled by teams of two or four horses, were raced 12 laps. Up to 40 chariots could take part in one race, so collisions were inevitable.

This life-size bronze statue of a horse and boy jockey was found in a shipwreck.

INTERNET LINKS

For links to websites where you can watch the ancient Games and see how they've changed, go to
www.usborne-quicklinks.com

WRESTLING AND BOXING

There were three types of wrestling events: upright wrestling, ground wrestling, which lasted longer, and a highly dangerous combination of wrestling and boxing, called the *pankration*. This could last for several hours, and absolutely any tactic, apart from biting and eye-gouging, was allowed. The boxers wore leather straps with metal studs, and they could make a terrible mess of their opponents. Some of them died.

The scene on this Greek vase shows two men engaging in upright wrestling.

The running events took place in the stadium. About 40,000 spectators could watch from embankments around the track.

This is the hippodrome, a large oval-shaped racetrack, where chariot and horse races were held.

THE WINNERS

After each event, a herald announced the name of the winner, but prizes were not awarded until the last day. The prizes, which were simple laurel wreaths, were only meant to be symbolic. The real prize lay in competing and in the glory of winning. Huge celebrations were held when the winners returned home. A victorious athlete won prestige for his city, and he was often handsomely rewarded by the city itself.

RELIGION AND MYTHOLOGY

The ancient Greeks had dozens of different gods and goddesses, each in charge of a different aspect of life or death, as well as many figures who were spirits, and some who were half-gods. Although the Greeks were very religious, they didn't follow a strict set of rules, as modern religions often do. People worshipped the gods they found most useful.

MYTHS AND LEGENDS

Myths were an important part of ancient Greek religion. Many myths were tales of the lives of the gods and their dealings with humans. Others were stories which explained natural phenomena, such as why day turned into night, why the seasons changed, or how the world began. Now, many of these ideas would be explained scientifically.

THE CREATION

According to legend, before anything existed, there was a nothingness called Chaos. Out of this dark and empty state, Gaea, Mother Earth, slowly emerged to form the world. She gave birth to Uranus, the sky.

Aphrodite - the goddess of love

THE FAMILY OF GIANTS

Gaea and Uranus married and had many children. The most important were the Titans, who looked like humans but were vast in size. They were the first gods and goddesses.

Uranus banished some of his children to the Underworld, a dark, gloomy place under the Earth. Gaea was furious, and encouraged the Titans to rise up against him. Led by Cronos, they attacked and overthrew their father.

This is a carving of Gaea, mother earth goddess

THE BIRTH OF ZEUS

Cronos then became King of the Titans. He married his sister Rhea and they had five children. Before the children were born, Cronos was warned that one of them would kill him. So he snatched and swallowed each baby at birth. Then, when Rhea was giving birth to her sixth baby, Zeus, she tricked Cronos by giving him a stone wrapped in clothes instead of the baby. So, Zeus survived.

THE REVENGE OF ZEUS

When he was fully grown, Zeus visited his parents in disguise, and slipped a potion into Cronos's drink. This made him cough up all the babies he had swallowed: his two sons, Poseidon and Pluto, and his daughters: Hera, Hestia and Demeter.

 INTERNET LINKS

For links to websites where you can try online games and quizzes about Greek gods and find out more about them, go to www.usborne-quicklinks.com

This photograph shows the summit of Mount Olympus, in Greece, where the gods were supposed to live.

THE NEW GODS

This carving from Delphi c.525BC shows the battle between the gods and giants.

The new Greek gods were known as Olympians, because people believed they inhabited a land high above the clouds on Mount Olympus. They lived like a large family, with Zeus as the head. No humans could visit Olympus, except by special invitation. The gods often visited the Earth, though. Sometimes they even fell in love with humans, and had children with them. Many heroes in Greek myths were born in this way and were half-human and half-god.

Zeus then led his brothers and sisters in revolt against Cronos and the other Titans. After a bitter struggle, the younger gods defeated the older ones and divided the world among themselves. Zeus became ruler of the sky and King of all the gods, with Hera as his queen. Poseidon was King of the Ocean; Pluto, King of the Underworld; Hestia, goddess of the hearth and home; and Demeter, goddess of plants and harvests.

This scene from a vase painting shows Pluto, god of the Underworld, and Persephone, Demeter's daughter.

This giant bronze statue of Poseidon, god of the sea, was found in the Aegean. The eyes are missing, but they would have been inlaid with jewels or semi-precious stones.

TEMPLES AND WORSHIP

Ancient Greek temples were not built for people to worship in, like churches, synagogues and mosques. The Greeks thought of them as somewhere for the gods and goddesses to live comfortably when they visited Earth. So each temple was dedicated to a particular god or goddess.

This shows a woman being carried off by the god Zeus, disguised as an eagle, on one of his visits to Earth.

TEMPLE DESIGN

The design of a Greek temple was based on the royal halls in the palaces of Mycenae. The early ones were just a simple room, called a cella, with a statue of the god or goddess. Later, temples became much more sophisticated. The largest and most ornate ones were built in the Classical Period.

This is a Greek pottery model of a Dark Age temple. Temples at this time were made of wood or mud brick, and consisted of a single room, called a cella.

This stone temple is from the Archaic Period. It had a porch at the front and at the back.

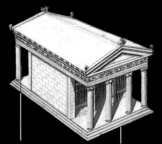

Back porch, or oisthodomus

Front porch, or pronaos

This a more sophisticated, Late Archaic Period temple. It had several steps up to the entrance, and a covered row of columns, called a peristyle, around the outside.

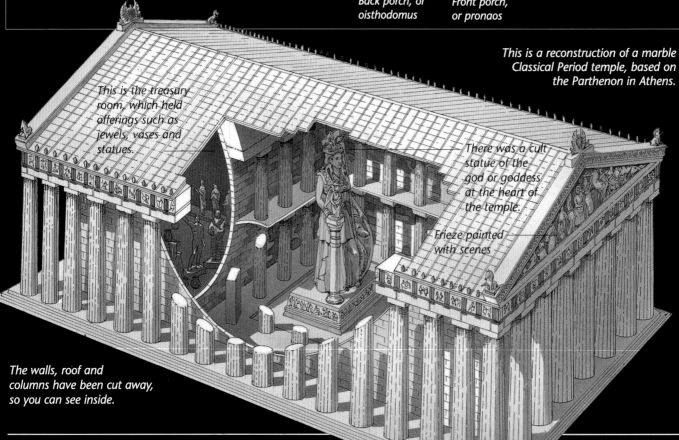

This is the treasury room, which held offerings such as jewels, vases and statues.

This is a reconstruction of a marble Classical Period temple, based on the Parthenon in Athens.

There was a cult statue of the god or goddess at the heart of the temple.

Frieze painted with scenes

The walls, roof and columns have been cut away, so you can see inside.

DAILY PRAYER

Religion played an important part in daily life. Greek families began the day with prayers at an altar in the courtyard of their house. During the prayers, they poured a libation (an offering of wine) over the altar.

Who they prayed to depended on what they were doing that day. For example, someone going on a journey would pray to Hermes, god of voyagers. A person with a special request would go to the temple of the appropriate god to make an offering.

This carving shows a procession of people making offerings to Demeter, goddess of harvests.

FOLLOWING THE RULES

Although religion was informal, there were strict rules on how to pray. Gods and goddesses had their own priests, who made sure the rules were followed correctly. If they weren't, the god might be offended, and the prayers rejected.

Different gods preferred offerings of different animals, and the rules about how the animal was to be killed, or sacrificed, varied too. For praying, the right appearance and gesture were of great importance.

Most gods were addressed with raised arms and hands turned up toward Heaven.

This marble statue is not from ancient Greece, but it shows the influence of the Greeks - both in style and subject.

It was made by a 16th century Italian artist named Michelangelo. The figure is supposed to combine the Greek god Apollo with David from the Bible.

INTERNET LINKS

For links to websites where you can make a model temple and see an animation, go to www.usborne-quicklinks.com

To address a sky god, the worshipper had to face the East.

For Underworld gods the worshipper's palms had to face the ground.

For a marine god, the worshipper had to face the sea.

TALKING TO THE GODS

The Greeks held festivals at various times right through the year, to pay respect to their gods, and persuade them to grant people's wishes, such as providing a good harvest, or winning a victory in war. Festivals were much more than just religious ceremonies: plays, music, dancing, athletic events and good food played a large part too. Some were small local events, but others drew crowds from miles around.

This sculpture shows water carriers at the festival of Athene in Athens. It is taken from a frieze on the Parthenon.

This woman, shown on a Greek vase painting, is bringing offerings to an altar.

THE GREAT FESTIVAL OF ATHENE

One of the most important dates in the Greek calendar was the Panathenaea, the festival held in Athens for Athene, patron goddess of the city. It took place each year, in the Greek month of Hekatombion (July/August), but every four years, it was celebrated on a much grander scale. Then, it lasted six whole days and was known as the Great Panathenaea

The celebrations began with music and singing, followed by athletic competitions, called the Panathenaic Games. The winners were presented with pots of the finest olive oil, from Athene's sacred olive tree. A grand procession led up to the Acropolis, where 100 cattle were slaughtered as an offering, and a magnificent new dress was draped around the statue of the goddess.

 INTERNET LINKS

*For a link to a website where you can have a look at the sacred site of Delphi, go to **www.usborne-quicklinks.com***

ORACLES AND OMENS

For major decisions, the Greeks always sought the advice of the gods. One way was to consult an oracle. An oracle could be a priestess who spoke for a god, the holy place where this happened, or the message she gave.

The most famous oracle was at Delphi, where the god Apollo was believed to speak through his priestess, called the Pythia. The Delphi oracle was so well-known that many Greek states sent delegations there for political advice.

Another skilled art, only undertaken by trained priests, was reading signs, or omens. An omen could be seen in such things as the entrails of sacrificed animals, the flight patterns of birds, or in flashes of lightning and earth tremors.

SOOTHSAYERS

Soothsayers were people who were thought to be able to see into the future. One famous and tragic example in Greek legend was the Trojan princess Cassandra, who was punished by Apollo for breaking a promise. He gave her the power to see the future, while ensuring that no one would believe her. When she warned the Trojans about the dangers of the wooden horse, they ignored her with fateful consequences: their city was destroyed by the Greeks.

This is a painting of the god Dionysus, subject of one of the wilder mystery cults.

MYSTERY CULTS

People who wanted a deeper religious experience could join a mystery cult, a group of people dedicated to a particular god. Members had to undergo strict training, including purification rituals and processions at night. Once admitted to the cult, they were sworn to secrecy, so no one is really sure what was involved.

These are the ruins of the temple of Apollo at Delphi, site of the most famous oracle.

DEATH AND THE UNDERWORLD

The ancient Greeks believed that when they died their souls were taken to Pluto's kingdom, known as Hades, or the Underworld. It was supposed to lie deep under the Earth's surface. People thought caves and cracks in the ground were doors leading into this secret world.

DRIFTING AWAY

The god Hermes guided the dead person's soul through one of these entrances, down to the banks of a river called the Styx. This marked the boundary between the worlds of the living and the dead. People were buried with a coin to pay the ferryman, whose name was Charon, to take them across the river. Once across the water, they were met by a three-headed dog called Cerberus.

This is an imaginary view of the Underworld, painted by a 16th century artist from the Netherlands.

His duty was to keep the living out of the Underworld, and prevent dead souls from escaping. Next, they reached a crossroads, where their destinies would be decided. Three judges inspected the new arrivals and directed them to one of three places: the Elysian Fields, the Asphodel Fields, or Tartarus.

Cerberus, from a Greek vase

The next life could be blissful, horrifying, or just plain dull. It all depended on how the person had behaved when he or she was alive.

The lucky few, who had led good and blameless lives, were allowed to enter the Elysian Fields: a happy place full of sunshine, warmth and laughter.

The wicked ones were flung into Tartarus, where they were condemned to eternal punishment, pain and misery.

Most people ended up in the Asphodel Fields, a drab and misty place, where the inhabitants drifted around aimlessly. The only relief from boredom came when they received offerings from their living relatives.

 INTERNET LINKS

For links to websites where you can play an Underworld myth game and see a movie about gravestones, go to **www.usborne-quicklinks.com**

LOVE AND DEATH

This is a Roman mosaic from Turkey, showing Orpheus, a character from a Greek myth, playing his lyre to some wild animals.

A well-known Greek myth tells of two lovers, Orpheus and Eurydice, who were separated and then joined by death. Orpheus was famed as the best musician in all of Greece. When Eurydice died from a snake bite, he went to the Underworld to beg Pluto to give her back. The god was so impressed when Orpheus played his lyre that he agreed to free Eurydice - but on one vital condition: Orpheus must not look at her - even once - on their journey back to the land of the living. But the temptation was too much for him. As Orpheus turned to gaze at her, Eurydice disappeared forever. He was so upset that he refused to play any more happy music. This made the gods so angry they sent creatures called Maenads to tear him to pieces. So, he was finally able to join his beloved in the Underworld.

FUNERALS AND BURIALS

When it came to the customs and rituals surrounding funerals and burials, the ancient Greeks were careful to follow very strict rules. They believed this was essential to make sure the dead person's soul reached the Underworld. For, without a proper funeral, the soul would wander lost and forgotten forever.

Pottery figure of woman holding her head in grief

BEFORE BURIAL

First, the dead person's body was washed, rubbed with perfumed oils, and dressed in white robes. Then, it was laid out for a day, so friends and relatives could come and pay their respects. A coin was put in its mouth, to pay the ferryman for the journey to the Underworld. Anyone buried without a coin was doomed to remain in this world as a ghost.

Mourners wore black clothes, cut their hair short, and displayed their grief very noisily. They cried and moaned and clapped their hands to show how sad they were.

This long-necked vase, called a loutrophoros, shows mourners weeping.

THE PROCESSION

Before dawn the next day, the body was taken away for burial. It was carried on the shoulders of male relatives or, if the family was rich enough, transported on a horse-drawn carriage. The procession was accompanied by friends and family, crying and wailing. To amplify the sounds of grief, rich families sometimes hired professional mourners to make even more noise at the funeral.

Offerings to the dead were left in pots, like this one.

AT THE TOMB

The dead were either buried or cremated in cemeteries outside the city walls, where each family had its own plot of land. Personal belongings were usually buried with the corpse, as well as food and drink for use in the afterlife.

Even after death, the family was expected to look after its ancestors by making offerings of food. This was done at birthdays and anniversaries, and at festivals for the dead.

This illustration of a dead person being visited by relatives comes from a Greek pot.

MACEDONIA
AND THE
HELLENISTIC
WORLD

These Corinthian columns from a Roman temple at Heliopolis (now Baalbek) near Damascus, show lasting Greek influence in the area conquered by Alexander the Great.

THE RISE OF MACEDONIA

The ancient kingdom of Macedonia lay in the northeast part of Greece. In Classical times, most Greeks regarded it as a culturally and politically backward place, inhabited by people who were little better than barbarians. They would scarcely have believed it would be possible that, in the 4th century BC, Macedonia would become the greatest military power of the day, posing a serious threat to Athenian democracy and independence.

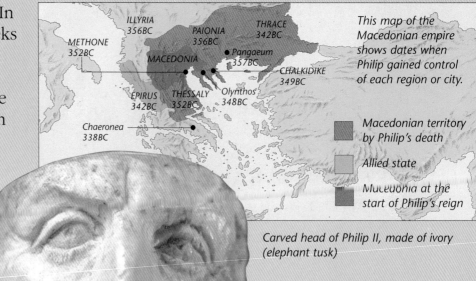

This map of the Macedonian empire shows dates when Philip gained control of each region or city.

- Macedonian territory by Philip's death
- Allied state
- Macedonia at the start of Philip's reign

Carved head of Philip II, made of ivory (elephant tusk)

ORDER OUT OF CHAOS

Macedonia had had an unstable history. It was invaded repeatedly in the 6th and 5th centuries BC, and in 399BC the country collapsed into civil war after the murder of its king. Decades of turmoil ended in 359BC, when Philip II became king and set about restoring order. Once he was firmly in control of his new kingdom, Philip began expanding his frontiers through military campaigns, taking over the regions to the east and south.

By 342BC, Philip had extended Macedonia to include all of Thrace, Chalkidike and Thessaly. Meanwhile, the other Greek states, led by Athens and Thebes, were growing very nervous of this rising power in the north. So, in 342BC, they formed the Hellenic League against Macedonia.

THE COLLAPSE OF THE CITY-STATES

In 338BC, Philip won a decisive victory against the Hellenic League at Chaeronea. This gave him control of Greece and marked the end of the city-states. He united the states into the League of Corinth, with himself as leader. To strengthen their unity, he planned an attack on the Persians.

The head (right) and butt (left) of a Macedonian spear

THE NEW ARMY

Philip reorganized the Macedonian army, making it the most efficient in Greece. It was led by elite units of foot soldiers and horsemen, called the Companions. Philip gave his troops heavier fighting clothes and long spears, and trained them in a particularly effective version of the phalanx (see page 43).

INTERNET LINKS

For a link to a website where you can play a game based on Philip's tomb, go to **www.usborne-quicklinks.com**

A carving of one of Philip's mounted bodyguards, the Companion Cavalry

PHILIP'S ASSASSINATION

Philip had several wives but only one queen, Olympias, mother of his heir, Alexander. In 337BC, Philip took another wife, replacing Olympias as queen. The next year, Philip was murdered, as he was about to attack the Persians. The killer might have been paid by the Persians, or by Olympias.

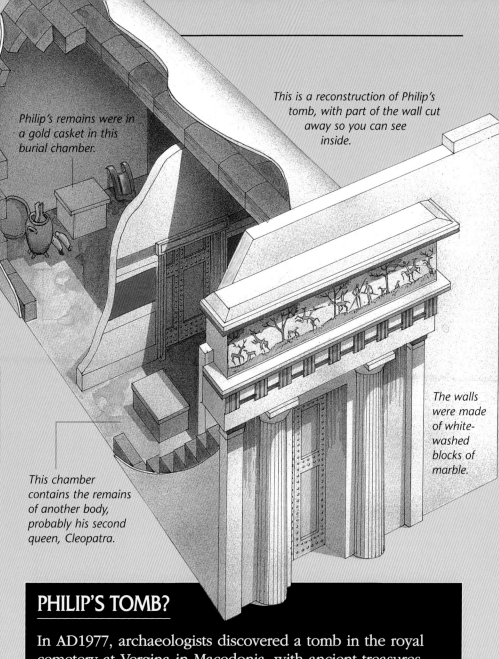

This is a reconstruction of Philip's tomb, with part of the wall cut away so you can see inside.

Philip's remains were in a gold casket in this burial chamber.

The walls were made of white-washed blocks of marble.

This chamber contains the remains of another body, probably his second queen, Cleopatra.

PHILIP'S TOMB?

In AD1977, archaeologists discovered a tomb in the royal cemetery at Vergina in Macedonia, with ancient treasures still inside it. Many scholars now believe this was Philip's tomb. In one room, archaeologists found a gold casket containing the cremated remains (bones as well as ashes) of a middle-aged man. His reconstructed skull had a wound near the right eye. As Philip is known to have lost his right eye in battle, experts think that these were almost certainly Philip's remains.

This gold casket held Philip's bones and ashes.

ALEXANDER THE GREAT

When Alexander became King of Macedonia in 336BC, he was only 20. Despite his youth, he immediately embarked on a military campaign that won him the greatest empire the world had ever seen and earned him the title "Alexander the Great". He was a military genius of extraordinary energy and courage, who inspired great loyalty in his soldiers.

This Ancient Roman mosaic, from Pompeii in Italy, shows Alexander on horseback at the Battle of Issus.

VICTORY OVER PERSIA

Alexander continued the task of expanding Macedonian territory that his father had begun. In 334BC, he led 35,000 soldiers into Asia Minor and set out to destroy the Persian army. He beat the Persian rulers of Asia Minor at the Battle of Granicus, and went on to defeat Darius III, the Persian king, at the Battle of Issus in 333BC. Darius fled and Alexander marched on to Egypt, where he overpowered the Persian governors and was crowned King of Egypt. But his greatest battle was yet to come. In 331BC, he destroyed the entire Persian army at Gaugamela. Once again, Darius escaped, but the Greeks pursued him and he was finally murdered by his own troops. Alexander was crowned Great King of Persia.

BUILDING AN EMPIRE

Alexander's army marched over 8,000 km (5,000 miles) and acquired an empire that stretched as far as northern India. Along the way, he founded several cities, including Alexandria in Egypt (see page 110).

INTERNET LINKS

For links to websites where you can watch movies and find out more about Alexander, go to **www.usborne-quicklinks.com**

This photograph shows the landscape of the Indus Valley, in northern India. It still looks much as it would have when Alexander's troops got there.

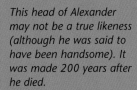

This head of Alexander may not be a true likeness (although he was said to have been handsome). It was made 200 years after he died.

This map shows the extent of Alexander's empire.

☐ Alexander's empire

➤ Alexander's route to India

Granicus
Issus · Gaugamela
Alexandria
PERSIA
EGYPT
INDIA

LOCAL RULE

Alexander had never planned to build an empire - only to rid himself of the Persian threat. The more land he acquired, the more he realized he couldn't control it from Greece. He replaced local rulers with Greek ones, but otherwise tried to cooperate with the local people. He wore Persian clothes and married a Persian woman named Roxane.

THE END OF AN ERA

Alexander's soldiers won every battle they fought, but by the time they reached India many of them refused to go on. So Alexander turned back to Persia with part of his army. In 323BC, they reached Babylon, but he caught a fever and died, aged only 32.

ALEXANDER'S ARMY

Alexander had inherited a highly efficient army from his father. The main part, known as the Royal Army, was from Macedonia, but there were soldiers from other states in the League of Corinth too, and professional soldiers from other parts of Greece.

CAVALRY AND INFANTRY

Alexander's cavalry was made up of 5,000 horsemen, mostly from the horse-breeding plains of Thessaly, led by the elite Companion Cavalry (see page 105). His infantry consisted of 30,000 foot soldiers, some armed with spears, others with javelins, bows and arrows or slings and stones.

The cavalry was divided into units of 49 men. Each unit charged in a wedge-shape, to break up a phalanx of enemy foot soldiers. His foot soldiers moved in from behind to finish off the enemy with hand-to-hand fighting.

THE HELLENISTIC WORLD

For several hundred years after Alexander's death, the territories of his former empire remained influenced by Greek culture. They are often described as the Hellenistic World, from the word *Hellene*, meaning 'Greek'. The period until the Roman conquest in 30BC (see page 114) is known as the Hellenistic Age.

This gold Hellenistic diadem, or headband, was made in Apulia, Italy in the 3rd century BC.

AFTER ALEXANDER

As news of Alexander's death reached Greece, rebellions broke out in many Greek cities, which turned into a full-scale war. After a year, the revolt was subdued by

Ptolemy III, a descendent of one of Alexander's generals

soldiers from Alexander's army returning from Asia. The empire itself was officially inherited by Alexander's infant son and half-brother Philip Arrideus, but it was ruled on their behalf by his generals, known as the Diadochi, meaning "successors".

THE EMPIRE DIVIDES

As rival Diadochi fought to grab the lion's share, the political unity of the empire was soon shattered by a terrible power struggle. By 301BC, Alexander's mother, wife, son and half-brother had all been murdered in the conflict. By 281BC, three separate kingdoms emerged from the chaos. They were ruled by descendants of three Diadochi: Antigonas, Seleucus and Ptolemy.

INTERNET LINKS

For links to websites where you can find interactive timelines of ancient Greece and examine artifacts of the Hellenistic world, go to www.usborne-quicklinks.com

HELLENISTIC ART

Although the peoples of Alexander's empire preserved their own culture and worshipped their own gods, Greek art and architecture often had an influence, even in places far from Greece. Statues of the Buddha from Gandhara in northern India show elements of style that are Greek, rather than traditionally Indian.

The features on this carving of the Buddha, including the expression, the tilt of the head and the curly hair, show signs of Greek influence.

Black Sea

Caspian Sea

ASIA MINOR

Mediterranean Sea

EGYPT

Map of the Hellenistic World in c.240BC

Kingdom of Ptolemy

Kingdom of Antigonas

Kingdom of Seleucus

Independent Greek states

THE ANTIGONIDS

Antigonas founded a new Greek dynasty, the Antigonids, who ruled from Macedonia. They kept the rest of Greece under their control by maintaining garrisons of soldiers in the main cities. In the 3rd century BC, however, the Greek colonies in southern Italy were threatened by the Romans, who were pursuing a policy of aggressive expansion. The Antigonids were soon dragged into a fatal series of wars with Rome.

THE SELEUCIDS

The ambitious leader Seleucus seized a huge part of Alexander's empire in the Middle East and Central Asia, but it was so big that his successors were never able to control it properly. Large parts soon began to break away. Wars, rebellions and disputes between the leaders of the Seleucid family all helped to weaken their hold on their dwindling empire.

THE PTOLEMIES

The dynasty founded by Ptolemy was in many ways the most successful of the three. He only took charge of Egypt, a relatively small portion of Alexander's empire. As a result, he was able to keep his kingdom intact for longer. Ptolemy also won great prestige by having Alexander's body buried in Alexandria, the Ptolemaic capital. Eventually, however, quarrels over the succession, and the expanding Roman empire, brought this final Greek dynasty to an end.

Even under Greek rule, the Egyptians continued to build in their own style. The temple at Kom Ombo (shown here, as it looks today) is entirely Egyptian in design.

ALEXANDRIA

When Alexander the Great arrived in Egypt in 332BC, he ordered the building of a new capital city, to be named after him, on the Mediterranean coast. Although he died before he was able to see it, the city of Alexandria became one of the leading cities in the ancient world.

CITY OF CULTURE

Alexandria owed its fame and prestige to outstanding achievements in science and scholarship. In the 3rd century BC, the Greek ruler, Ptolemy II, founded the first 'museum' - not a museum in the modern sense, but a temple to the Muses, nine goddesses of the arts and sciences. Next to the temple was a huge library, with writings from Greece, Egypt and beyond.

Over several centuries, around half a million works were collected in the library. After Greek civilization declined (see page 114), this collection played a big part in preserving knowledge of Classical Greece for future generations.

THE PHAROS

Probably the greatest building in all Alexandria was a fabulous marble lighthouse, called the Pharos, overlooking the city's busy port. Named by ancient writers as one of the Seven Wonders of the World (see right), it stood until the 14th century AD, when it was destroyed by earthquakes. In 1480, some of its stones were used to build an Arab fort

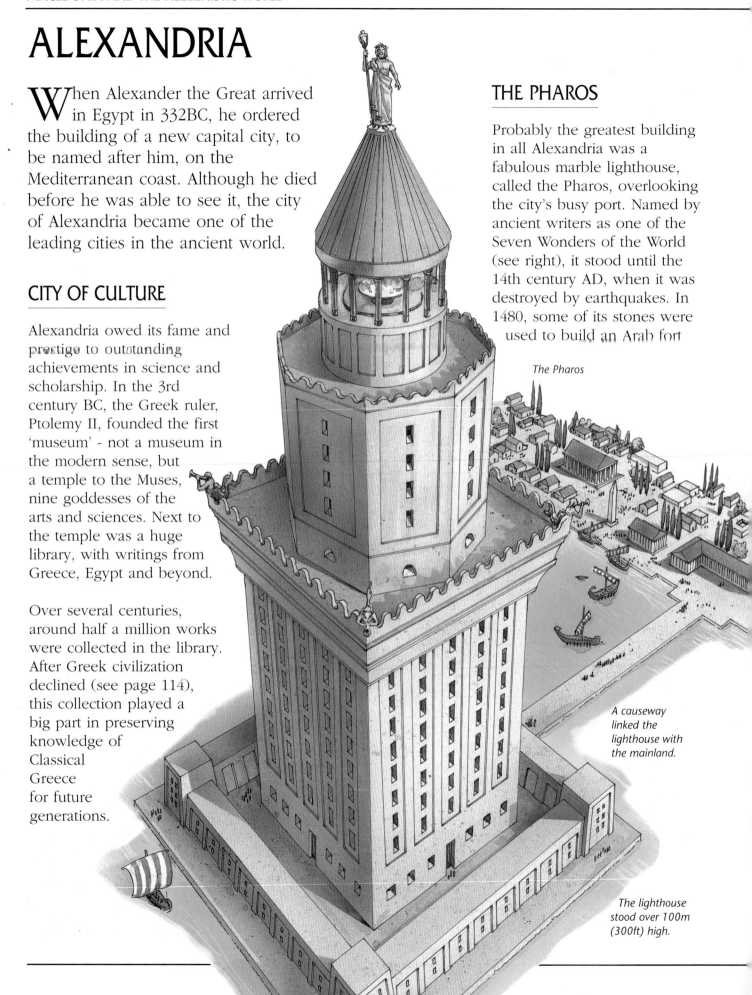

The Pharos

A causeway linked the lighthouse with the mainland.

The lighthouse stood over 100m (300ft) high.

THE SEVEN WONDERS

Great feats of engineering and architecture captured the imaginations of people in ancient times - just as they do today. The greatest of these were the famous monuments which the Greeks called 'the Seven Wonders of the World'. Only one of the seven survives, so we have to rely to some extent on written accounts to give an impression of what they looked like.

 INTERNET LINKS

For links to websites where you can watch underwater discoveries in Alexandria and play a game about the Seven Wonders, go to **www.usborne-quicklinks.com**

The Seven Wonders of the Ancient World

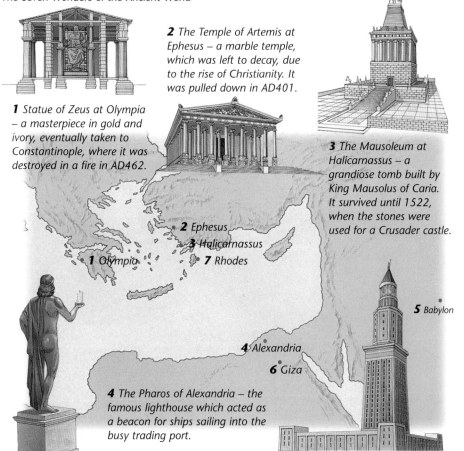

1 *Statue of Zeus at Olympia – a masterpiece in gold and ivory, eventually taken to Constantinople, where it was destroyed in a fire in AD462.*

2 *The Temple of Artemis at Ephesus – a marble temple, which was left to decay, due to the rise of Christianity. It was pulled down in AD401.*

3 *The Mausoleum at Halicarnassus – a grandiose tomb built by King Mausolus of Caria. It survived until 1522, when the stones were used for a Crusader castle.*

2 *Ephesus*
3 *Halicarnassus*
1 *Olympia*
7 *Rhodes*
5 *Babylon*
4 *Alexandria*
6 *Giza*

4 *The Pharos of Alexandria – the famous lighthouse which acted as a beacon for ships sailing into the busy trading port.*

7 *The Colossus of Rhodes – a huge statue, of legendary dimensions, that straddled the entrance to the port. It was damaged in an earthquake in 226BC and then sold to a Syrian trader.*

6 *The Great Pyramid at Giza. Built as a tomb for Egyptian Pharaoh Khufu, this is the only one of the Seven Wonders that is still standing.*

5 *The Hanging Gardens of Babylon – beautiful terraced gardens that adorned the city of Babylon during the 6th century BC.*

IN SEARCH OF THE LIGHTHOUSE

In 1994, a team of archaeologists began to explore the port of Alexandria, hoping to find evidence of the celebrated lighthouse. Divers examined huge piles of debris, and made an accurate map of the seabed.

Most of the underwater discoveries predated the Greek arrival in Egypt. But there was a giant statue and some massive blocks of stone that were from the right era.

Archaeologists believe the statue is very likely to be Ptolemy II, and that the stone blocks could be all that is left of the illustrious lighthouse, lost to the world for five centuries.

This diver may be gazing into the eyes of a statue of Ptolemy II.

INQUIRING MINDS

The ancient Greeks were responsible for many of the ideas about art, literature, philosophy, science, politics and history that laid the foundations of European civilization. From about the 6th century BC, scholars began to ask questions and make observations about the world around them. The people who did this are known as philosophers, from the Greek word *philosophos*, meaning 'lover of wisdom'.

This is a carved head of Plato, one of the most famous Athenian philosophers.

PHILOSOPHY

For the ancient Greeks, philosophy wasn't just the study of ideas about the meaning of life. It covered almost everything - from every branch of science to moral questions, such as how people should behave and what an ideal political system would be.

EVOLUTION

One scholar, Anaximander, concluded that much of the Earth had once been covered in water, and that people had developed from other animals - possibly fish. Another scholar, Xenophanes, discovered that fossils were the remains of plants and animals preserved in rock.

This drawing shows a model of an early steam machine, designed by Hero, a Greek from Alexandria. Fire boiled the water inside a metal ball. Steam escaped, which made the ball rotate.

This medieval manuscript is supposed to show Aristotle, one of the great Athenian philosophers, teaching Alexander the Great.

HISTORY

When the Greeks were involved in the Persian Wars, they realized the importance of knowing more about their enemies. They began to keep records of their history, and that of other peoples.

The first real historian was probably Herodotus, often described as the 'father of history'. Herodotus wrote an account of the Persian Wars after interviewing survivors to find out what had actually happened. Most earlier histories were far less accurate.

INTERNET LINKS

*For links to websites where you can find out about ancient Greek thinkers, inventors and achievements, go to **www.usborne-quicklinks.com***

MATHEMATICS AND PHYSICS

Many basic mathematical rules were first thought out by Greek scholars, such as Euclid, Pythagoras and Archimedes. Pythagoras devised a theorem for calculating the size of the angles in triangles and introduced the symbol p for determining the area and the circumference of a circle.

MEDICINE

The first "doctors" were priests of Asclepius, the god of healing. Sick people visited one of his temples, where priests tried to cure them with prayers. The first man to adopt a more practical, scientific approach was Hippocrates of Kos. He tried to search for the causes of illnesses and to find out how the body worked. His followers opened schools where his ideas were taught. They prescribed herbal medicines, a special diet, rest or exercise. They performed operations too - but without painkillers, so this was both dangerous and painful.

These pages are from Elements, a famous book by Euclid. Part of the book sums up the work of the mathematicians before him.

ASTRONOMY

An astronomer named Aristarchus reckoned that the Earth revolved on its axis and that it moved around the Sun. At this time, most people believed that the Sun moved around the Earth, and so his ideas were rejected as he had no evidence to prove them.

Archimedes discovered an important law of physics when he noticed that the water in his bath tub overflowed. From this, he deduced that an object displaces its own volume of water.

This is a demonstration of one of Archimedes' inventions: a large screw which acts as a water pump, raising water from one level to another.

Another astronomer, named Anaxagoras, realized that the Moon did not produce its own light, but reflected the light of the Sun. He also calculated that eclipses were caused by the Moon blocking the light as it passed between the Sun and the Earth.

THE ROMAN CONQUEST

While Alexander's inheritance was in political disarray, there was a formidable new power rising in the west: Rome. By 200BC, the Romans dominated much of Italy and were pushing their frontiers in all directions. It was just a matter of time before they would threaten the stability of the fragile Hellenistic kingdoms.

Although this portrait of Cleopatra VII was carved in Egyptian style, the Ptolemies kept their Greek culture. Cleopatra was the only ruler who learned the Egyptian language.

THE CONQUEST OF GREECE

At the end of a long series of wars against the Romans, the Antigonid rulers were defeated and removed from power in 168BC. Greece was split into Roman provinces in 147-146BC.

THE END OF THE SELEUCIDS

Meanwhile, the Seleucids were finding it impossible to control the vast, rambling territory they had inherited, and their empire was gradually falling apart. The final blow came in 64BC. After two years of successful campaigning, the Roman general Pompey conquered the remaining Seleucid territory and added it to the ever-expanding Roman empire.

ANTONY AND CLEOPATRA

The face on this coin is Mark Antony.

The fate of Ptolemaic Egypt was caught up in a power struggle between two Roman leaders: Octavian and Mark Antony, who was having an affair with the Queen of Egypt, Cleopatra VII. Octavian defeated them in a sea battle at Actium in 31BC and landed in Alexandria the following year. Antony and Cleopatra committed suicide and the last of Alexander's kingdoms fell into Roman hands.

THE GRAECO -ROMAN WORLD

Although the Romans were the conquerors, they were greatly influenced by Greek ideas and culture. So many aspects of Greek art, architecture, religion and customs survived, even after the Hellenistic Age. Greek remained a major language, and cities like Athens became financial and administrative bases within the Roman empire.

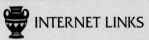

INTERNET LINKS

For links to websites where you can explore an online exhibit about Cleopatra and read how the Greeks influenced Roman culture, go to **www.usborne-quicklinks.com**

These are Roman legionaries, the well-trained soldiers who conquered a huge empire.

FACTFINDER

Statue of a young woman holding
a tray with sacrificial objects,
probably Greek, 2nd century BC.

GODS AND GODDESSES

The ancient Greeks believed in many different gods and goddesses, sometimes described as Immortals, each one concerned with particular aspects of life or death. People thought of them as being very like humans, with feelings such as love, hate, or anger. Here are the most important ones. In brackets, you can see how to pronounce their names.

AEOLUS (ee-oh-luss)
Aeolus was the keeper of the winds. He was usually helpful, but was sometimes unable to keep the winds under control.

APHRODITE (aff-ro-die-tee)
Aphrodite, the daughter of Uranus and wife of Hephaestos, was the goddess of love and beauty. She was born in the sea and rode to shore on a shell. Charming but vain, she had many admirers because of her great beauty.
One of them was Ares, which made Hera very jealous. Aphrodite was thought to have provoked the Trojan War, by promising Helen, the wife of Menelaus, to Paris, if he judged her the most beautiful goddess. Her symbols were roses, doves, sparrows, dolphins and rams.

APOLLO (a-poll-o)
Apollo was the god of the Sun, light and truth, and controlled the Sun's movement across the sky. Apollo was also patron of the Arts and was a skilled musician. He was the twin brother of Artemis, and very protective of his mother and sister. He killed his mother's enemy, the serpent Python, when it was sheltering in the shrine at Delphi, and made Delphi his Oracle. His symbol was a laurel tree.

ARES (air-eez)
Ares was the god of war. He had a violent temper and was always picking fights. He was young, strong and handsome, and an expert but jealous lover.
He once had to stand trial for murder in Athens, on the hill of the Areopagus, which was named after him. His symbols were a burning torch, a spear, dogs and vultures.

ARTEMIS (are-tem-iss)
Artemis was the moon goddess and huntress. She never married, was fiercely independent and could be merciless in her vengeance. Her silver arrows brought plague and death, but she also had healing powers. She protected young girls and pregnant women and was the mistress of wild animals. Her symbols were cypress trees, deers and dogs.

ASCLEPIUS (ass-klep-ee-us)
Asclepius, the god of medicine, was the son of Apollo and Coronis. He had been a mortal and a very successful doctor. But he went too far by bringing the dead back to life. He was killed by Zeus and then revived to become a god himself.

ATHENE (a-thee-nee)
Athene was born from the head of Zeus after he swallowed the Titaness Metis in the form of a fly. Athene was the goddess of wisdom and war and the patron goddess of Athens. She rarely lost her temper, but if angered she could be deadly. Her symbols, also used by the city of Athens, were the owl and the olive tree.

DEMETER (de-meet-a)
Demeter was the goddess of the earth, plants and harvests. She was helped by her daughter, Persephone, but when Persephone was kidnapped by Pluto to be his wife, Demeter abandoned her duties to go in search of her. Her symbol was a sheaf of wheat or barley.

DIONYSUS (die-on-eye-sus)
Dionysus was born from the thigh of Zeus. He was the god of wine and plays. He journeyed around the world, teaching people how to make wine from grapes. He led a wild, pleasure-filled life, attended by fanatical followers, especially female creatures called Maenads. He became cup-bearer to the gods.

EOS (ee-oss)
Eos was goddess of the dawn, and made the Sun rise every morning when she drove her chariot across the skies. She had been cursed by Aphrodite to fall in love with many different men, after she had an affair with Aphrodite's lover, Ares.

ERIS (air-iss)

Eris was the daughter of Zeus and Hera, and goddess of spite. She was troublesome and vengeful and helped to cause all sorts of conflicts, including the Trojan War.

EROS (ear-oss)

Eros made couples fall in love, even if they were unsuited to each other. He could be mischievous, but got into trouble himself by falling in love with the mortal (human) Psyche, when he was accidentally grazed with his own arrow. The problem was solved when Zeus made Psyche immortal.

HEBE (hee-bee)

Hebe was the daughter of Zeus and Hera, and cup-bearer to the gods. She was thought to have married the Greek hero Heracles after he was made a god.

HEPHAESTOS (heff-eye-stoss)

Hephaestos, the patron of craftsmen, was hard-working, skilled at making things and kind, but life was unkind to him. As a child he was crippled after being thrown from Olympus by his bad-tempered mother, Hera. Aphrodite was forced to marry him against her will and he suffered ever after from her constant infidelities.

HERA (hear-a)

Hera was the daughter of Cronos and Rhea, and the sister and wife of Zeus. As the protector of women and marriage, she was proud and jealous, and spent much of her time chasing her husband's many lovers and punishing them in ingenious and cruel ways. Hera's symbols were the pomegranate and peacock.

HERMES (her-meez)

Hermes was energetic and mischievous as a child and stole cattle from Apollo. But he won Apollo's forgiveness by inventing the lyre and giving it to him. To keep him out of trouble, Zeus made him messenger to the gods, and patron of voyagers and thieves. He wore a winged hat and carried a staff with entwined snakes.

HESTIA (hess-tee-a)

Hestia, goddess of the hearth, was very popular, as she protected people's homes. Every family had a shrine dedicated to her. Hestia was quiet and gentle and did not get involved in the jealous quarrels that blew up all the time on Mount Olympus. She eventually gave up her place on Olympus to Dionysus.

PAN (pan)

Pan, son of Hermes, was god of nature, shepherds and sheep. He fell in love with a nymph (a type of lesser goddess) called Syrinx, but she escaped him by turning into a bed of reeds. Pan used them to make musical pipes to play on.

PERSEPHONE (per-seff-on-nee)

Persephone was the daughter of Zeus and Demeter, and helped her mother with growing things and harvests. She was kidnapped by Pluto to be Queen of the Underworld, but she was very unhappy. So a bargain was struck: she spent half the year with her mother (spring and summer), and half with Pluto (autumn and winter). According to the Greeks, this was the origin of the seasons.

PLUTO (plue-toe)

Pluto was the brother of Zeus and Hera, and King of the Underworld (beneath the Earth). He drove a gold chariot with black horses and guarded the dead jealously. Pluto was extremely rich, as he owned all the precious stones and metals inside the Earth. Persephone was his queen.

POSEIDON (poss-eye-don)

Poseidon was the brother of Zeus and Hera, and King of the Oceans. He lived in an underwater palace, rode a gold chariot with white horses, and controlled storms, sea monsters and earthquakes. His symbols were a trident, dolphins and horses.

URANUS (you-rain-us)

Uranus was the sky. He and Mother Earth created all living things, including some monstrous children. Heartless and cruel, he imprisoned some of his children and Mother Earth turned against him.

ZEUS (zyooss)

Zeus, the ruler of the gods, was married to his sister, Hera. He had one son and two daughters by her: Ares, Eris and Hebe. But his relationship with Hera was very explosive. This was because he had many love affairs with mortal (human) women, appearing to them in many different disguises - as a bull, a swan, or a shower of gold. His symbols were the thunderbolt, the eagle and the oak tree.

GREEK MYTHS

Myths are old, traditional stories which often try to explain the things that happen in the natural world. They usually involve the adventures of gods, goddesses and heroes. Ancient Greek myths are among the most famous in the world. As well as gods and heroes, they are full of monsters, magic and amazing feats. Many Greek plays (see pages 122-123) retold the traditional Greek myths, and to this day people still write plays, poems and even TV series based on the stories.

PROMETHEUS

Prometheus upset Zeus, the king of the gods, by teaching the gods' secrets to humans. He showed them how to grow crops, tame horses and use plants as medicines. When he gave humans the secret of fire, Zeus was furious and devised a terrible punishment. Prometheus was chained to a rock on Mount Caucasus, and every day a vulture came and tore out his liver. Every night, it grew back. After many years of this torture, Prometheus was finally rescued by Heracles (see opposite).

PANDORA'S BOX

Zeus created Pandora, the first woman, as a wife for Prometheus (see above). He asked Hephaestos, the blacksmith of the gods, to shape her out of clay, and then breathed life into her. He gave her a beautiful box, which he forbade her to open. But one day her curiosity overcame her, and she opened the lid. With a terrible rushing sound, out of the box flew all the evils of the world - sin, sickness, age and death. Finally, one last thing flew out. It was Hope, and it meant that despite these horrors, people should not despair.

PERSEPHONE

Demeter, the goddess of crops and harvests, had a beautiful daughter, Persephone. When Pluto, god of the Underworld, saw Persephone he fell in love with her and wanted to marry her. But nobody ever wanted to live in the Underworld, so he kidnapped Persephone.

Demeter was so upset that she neglected her duties and no crops grew. She begged Zeus to help her get Persephone back, but Zeus could only persuade Pluto to return her for half of each year. For the six months Persephone spent with her mother, Demeter was happy, and the sun shone and the crops grew. This became spring and summer. But when Persephone was in the Underworld, it became winter.

APOLLO AND DAPHNE

Apollo fell in love with a beautiful nymph (a kind of half-goddess) named Daphne. But she didn't want his attention, and she ran away, praying to Mother Earth to save her. Just as Apollo was about to catch her, her prayers were answered and she was turned into a laurel tree. From then on, Apollo wore a wreath of laurel leaves in her memory.

THE WEAVING CONTEST

Athene was the goddess of wisdom and war, and also of handicrafts. When a princess called Arachne boasted that she was an even better weaver than the goddess, Athene was so annoyed that she challenged Arachne to a contest. But her irritation turned to fury when she discovered that Arachne really could weave as beautifully as she could. Athene tore up Arachne's weaving, and Arachne was so frightened that she tried to hang herself. Ashamed of what she had done, Athene saved Arachne from death by turning her into a spider. Ever since, spiders have woven beautiful webs.

DAEDALUS AND ICARUS

Daedalus, a great Athenian inventor, was so jealous of his clever nephew Talos that he killed him. Then he fled with his son Icarus to Crete, to work for King Minos. He built the Labyrinth, a maze for a monster named the Minotaur to live in. But Minos turned against Daedalus, so he had to escape. He built wings out of feathers and wax for himself and Icarus and they flew away. But Icarus flew too near the Sun. The wax melted, his wings fell apart, and he fell into the sea and died. Daedalus landed at Cumae and built a temple.

THESEUS AND THE MINOTAUR

Theseus was the son of King Aegeus of Athens. Once a year the Athenians were forced to send fourteen young men and women to Crete as food for the Minotaur, a monster which lived in a maze called the Labyrinth, built by Daedalus (see above).

Theseus decided to sail to Crete with the victims to kill the Minotaur. He told his father that when he came home he would put white sails on his ship if he had been successful. If the ship had its usual black sails, Aegeus would know Theseus was dead.

In Crete, King Minos's daughter Ariadne fell in love with Theseus. She gave him a sword to kill the Minotaur and a ball of thread, which Theseus tied to the entrance of the Labyrinth to help him find his way out. He found the Minotaur, killed it and escaped. Then he, Ariadne and the other Athenians fled from Crete.

On the way back to Athens, they stopped at the island of Naxos. By now Theseus was bored of Ariadne and one night, when she was asleep, he set sail without her. The gods punished him for his cowardice by making him forget to hoist his white sails. Aegeus saw the black sails and, believing his son was dead, threw himself off a cliff. The sea where he died is now called the Aegean Sea.

PARIS AND THE TROJAN WAR

When the sea goddess Thetis married a human, Peleus, they did not invite Eris, the goddess of spite and discord. Furious, she turned up anyway with a golden apple. Written on it were the words "for the fairest". The goddesses Hera, Athene and Aphrodite started arguing about who should own it, so Zeus sent them to ask a Trojan shepherd boy, Paris, to judge which of them was the most beautiful. He chose Aphrodite. As a reward she told him that he would have the most beautiful woman in the world as his wife.

Years later, Paris went to compete in the games in Troy. He did so well that the king and queen asked to see him. They realized that he was their own son. A prophecy had said that he would cause the downfall of Troy, so they had had him sent away. But they were so glad to see him that they welcomed him back.

Paris was sent on a mission to visit Menelaus, King of Sparta in Greece. He fell in love with Menelaus's wife Helen, the most beautiful woman in the world. While Menelaus was away, Paris and Helen escaped to Troy.

This led to the Trojan War (see page 26). All Greece's armies sailed to Troy to get Helen back. After ten years of fighting, the Greeks won. Troy was destroyed, and many people were killed, including Paris and Achilles, the son of Thetis and Peleus. Helen was reunited with Menelaus and taken back to Sparta.

THE ODYSSEY

After the Trojan War, King Odysseus of Ithaca, one of the Greek leaders, set off for home. But his ships were blown off course and he wandered the seas for ten years. He met many monsters on his journey, or 'odyssey'. His men were killed, and he arrived home alone, to find his palace full of princes trying to force his wife Penelope to marry them. Odysseus killed the princes in a huge battle and reclaimed his kingdom.

AGAMEMNON

Agamemnon, King of Mycenae, led the Greek armies in the Trojan War. While Agamemnon was at Troy, his wife Clytemnestra, who hated her husband for sacrificing their daughter Iphigenia to help the Greeks win the war, fell in love with Aegisthus, Agamemnon's cousin and enemy. When Agamemnon came home, the couple pretended to welcome him as a hero but then murdered him.

Agamemnon's son Orestes, supported by his sister Electra, took revenge on the murderers by killing them both. But by killing his mother, Orestes had committed a terrible crime, and he went insane. At last, as he had suffered enough, the gods forgave him and he became the King of Mycenae.

HERACLES

Heracles, known as Hercules by the Romans, was the Greeks' most popular hero. He was the son of Zeus and a human named Alcmene. Zeus' wife Hera was jealous of Alcmene and so she tried to kill Heracles. When he was still a baby, she sent two deadly serpents to bite him in his cradle. But he amazed everyone by strangling the serpents with his bare hands.

Heracles married Megara, and became famous for his great strength and courage. But Hera was jealous of his happiness and drove him insane, so that he killed his wife and children. When he saw what he had done, he was horrified and asked the Oracle at Delphi how he could make amends. He was told to offer himself as a slave to King Eurystheus, who gave Heracles twelve "impossible" tasks (known as the Twelve Labours of Heracles) involving killing monsters and finding rare objects. If he was able do them all he would be cleansed of his guilt. With the help of the gods, Heracles succeeded and became immortal.

One of Heracles' tasks was to fight the Nemean Lion. He strangled the beast and wore its skin as a cloak.

OEDIPUS

Oedipus was the son of King Laius and Queen Jocasta of Thebes. An oracle predicted that Oedipus would kill his father and marry his mother, so he was left on a mountain to die. A shepherd found him and took him to Corinth where the king and queen adopted him. Years later, Oedipus heard the oracle's prophecy and ran away from Corinth, believing the king and queen were his real parents.

On the way to Thebes, he killed a stranger in a fight, not realizing that it was his real father Laius. Then, after solving a riddle and defeating a monster called the sphinx, he became King of Thebes and married the queen, Jocasta - his real mother. When the truth came out, Jocasta hanged herself in shame and Oedipus blinded himself. He fled from Thebes and died at Colonus.

PERSEUS AND THE GORGON

Perseus was the son of Zeus and a woman named Danae. Polydectes, King of Seriphos, sent him to kill Medusa, a gorgon. She had snakes for hair and her eyes could turn people to stone. But the gods helped Perseus, and Athene gave him a mirror so he wouldn't have to look directly at the gorgon. Perseus killed Medusa, cut off her head and gave it to Athene to stick in the middle of her shield.

ANDROMEDA

Andromeda was a beautiful princess, the daughter of King Cepheus of Ethiopia and his wife Cassiopeia. Cassiopeia boasted that Andromeda was more beautiful than the Nereids (sea nymphs, or half-goddesses), and they complained to the sea god Poseidon. He sent a sea-monster to ravage Cepheus's lands. An oracle told Cepheus to sacrifice Andromeda to the monster to stop the attacks, so she was tied to a rock by the seashore. The hero Perseus rescued her by turning the monster to stone, using the gorgon's head (see left). Then he married her.

JASON AND THE ARGONAUTS

Jason was the son of Aeson, the rightful King of Iolkos. When he grew up, Jason went to claim the throne of Iolkos from Aeson's brother Pelias, who had seized it. Pelias said Jason must first fetch the golden fleece, a magic ram's fleece which hung in the grove of Ares, guarded by a dragon. Jason took a ship, the *Argo*, and a band of heroes, the Argonauts, and set off to get the fleece. He married Medea, an enchantress, and she helped him win the fleece. But she then killed Pelias, and she and Jason had to leave Iolkos to escape Pelias's angry brother Acastus.

BELLEROPHON

Bellerophon was the son of King Glaucus of Corinth, and served at the court of another king, King Proteus of Argos. But unfortunately Proteus's wife, Anteia, fell in love with Bellerophon. When he rejected her, she was furious and told Proteus that Bellerophon was in love with her and wouldn't leave her alone. Proteus was angry and wanted to kill Bellerophon, but he didn't dare. Instead he sent Bellerophon to visit Iobates, the King of Lycia, with a sealed letter. The letter asked Iobates to kill Bellerophon.

However, when Iobates read the letter, he didn't want to commit murder either. Instead he sent Bellerophon to kill the Chimaera - a fierce, fire-breathing monster with a lion's head, a goat for a body, and a snake for a tail - knowing he would probably die. But the gods helped Bellerophon by lending him the magical winged horse, Pegasus. Riding on its back, Bellerophon managed to kill the Chimaera.

Then Proteus sent Bellerophon to fight the Solymi, a tribe of mighty warriors, and the Amazons, a tribe of fierce women, but he conquered them both. At last Bellerophon made friends with Iobates and married his daughter Philonoe.

Later, Bellerophon tried to fly to Mount Olympus, the home of the gods, on the back of Pegasus. Zeus, furious at his impudence, made Pegasus throw him off. Bellerophon became an outcast and died alone.

Bellerophon fighting the Chimaera on the back of his winged horse, Pegasus

GREEK PHILOSOPHY

Ancient Greek philosophers like Plato and Socrates are very famous. But what exactly was Greek philosophy?

In fact, philosophy (which is Greek for 'love of knowledge') is not as complicated as it sounds. In ancient Greece, it simply meant trying to explain how the world worked, and trying to decide how people should behave and how society should be run. Of course, different philosophers had different ideas. As time went on, different systems or 'schools' of philosophy developed. The most important ideas and schools are explained here.

THE EARLY THINKERS

Greek philosophy probably started in around 600BC in Ionia (the area of ancient Greece which is now part of Turkey), when **Thales of Miletus** developed a theory that the whole universe was made of water. It could appear in the form of objects, plants, animals and people, but these were all really just different types of water.

After Thales, **Anaximander** (c.610-545BC) also argued that everything was made of one substance - not water, but an everlasting force called the *apeiron*. Anaximander had some other ideas too - he said the Earth was drum-shaped, and that life had begun when mud was warmed by the Sun (which is not so far from what some scientists believe today). Another philosopher, **Anaximenes** (c.546BC), suggested the substance everything was made of was air.

However, all these early thinkers had one thing in common - they were trying to work out how the universe was constructed and what made it tick.

THE CULT OF PYTHAGORAS

Pythagoras (c.580-c.500BC) was a philosopher and religious leader. He thought that when people died, they were reincarnated (born again) as other people or animals. But he also had scientific ideas: he said that the Earth was a sphere, and that the way the universe worked was based on mathematics and the relationships between numbers. He had a large cult (group of followers) who passed on his ideas after he died. Many of Pythagoras's theories influenced other Greek philosophers and are also still important to our understanding of science today.

THE ELEATIC SCHOOL

Following on from **Anaximander**, several philosophers had new ideas about the force that made up the universe. **Xenophanes** (c.570BC-c.475BC) saw it as a great godlike being. **Parmenides** (c.515BC-c.445BC) argued that the changing, varied everyday world was just an illusion and that in fact the universe was constant and unchanging. His follower **Zeno** (c.490BC-c.440BC) claimed it was impossible for many different things to exist. 'Things' were just different aspects of one universe. This approach was called the **Eleatic School**, because Zeno and Parmenides lived in Elea in Italy.

ELEMENTS, SEEDS AND ATOMS

Some philosophers strongly disagreed with the Eleatic School. **Empedocles** (c.495BC-c.435BC) said that far from being one single thing, the universe was made up of four elements - air, earth, fire and water. **Anaxagoras** (c.500BC-c.428BC) had another view: he thought the universe was made up of tiny 'seeds' of different substances, while **Leucippus** (5th century BC) and **Democritus** (c.460BC-357BC) thought it was made up of invisible atoms. These philosophers are sometimes called the **atomists** or **pluralists**.

SOCRATES

A medieval illustration of a book by Aristotle

In Athens in the 5th century BC, **Socrates** (469BC-399BC) invented a new philosophy. He was concerned with *arete*, which means 'goodness'. He held sessions in which he questioned other people's ideas of what goodness really was. He also believed that being good made people happy. But Socrates upset politicians with all his questions, and was executed. After his death, his pupils wrote down his ideas and passed them on. The debate over what is good and what is bad became known as **ethics**.

PLATO

Plato (c.429-347BC) was a pupil of Socrates, but slowly developed his own ideas. Like Socrates, he was interested in the nature of goodness. He said that states should be run by 'philosopher-kings' who knew better than most people what goodness was. He is also famous for his theory of **ideals**. He said that an ideal version of each thing existed in a 'World of Ideas'. A real thing, such as a chair, a dog or a human, could never be as good as the ideal version, but humans could try to get nearer to ideals through philosophy. Plato's ideas spread across the world and are still important today.

ARISTOTLE

Aristotle (384BC-322BC) was Plato's pupil, but disagreed with him about ideals, which he did not believe in. However, he too thought that people could reach towards goodness by using the power of their minds, or *nous*, for thinking philosophical thoughts. Aristotle also wrote about many other subjects (see page 127).

GREEK PLAYS

Greek plays were mainly divided into tragedies, comedies and satyrs. Tragedies were meant to show people how or how not to behave. They often retold traditional stories about heroes and gods. Comedies were mostly funny and dealt with politics or the battle between men and women. Satyrs were rude, biting comedies, which mocked serious themes. However, tragedies could be funny too, and some even had happy endings.

Although hundreds of plays were written, only a few, including those by Aeschylus, Sophocles, Euripides and Aristophanes, survive. The plots of some of the most famous ones are summarized here.

ALCESTIS

This play by Euripides is a tragedy with a happy ending. Admetus has been granted a long life by the gods, as long as he can persuade someone else to die for him. His parents refuse, so his dutiful wife Alcestis dies for him instead. Admetus is very upset and regrets her death. When his friend, the hero Heracles, finds out what has happened, he goes to rescue Alcestis from the Underworld, and brings her back to life.

ANTIGONE

A tragedy by Sophocles. Antigone buries her brother Polyneices, who has died in a fight to win control of Thebes. King Creon, who has ordered that the body should not be buried, has Antigone left to die in a cave as punishment. Her fiancé, Creon's son Haemon, is outraged and leaves to go to her. Creon also goes to the cave, where he finds that Antigone has hanged herself. Haemon stabs himself to death. When Creon goes home, his wife Eurydice has also killed herself.

THE BIRDS

A comedy by Aristophanes. Two Athenians, Peisetairos and Euelpides, are looking for a better place to live. They persuade the birds to build a kingdom in the air, called Cloud-cuckooland. For food, they plan to steal sacrifices intended for the gods. All goes well until the goddess Iris comes to complain. Peisetairos demands Zeus's daughter Basilaeia as his wife in return for an agreement. At last the birds and the gods make peace, and Peisetairos replaces Zeus as king of the gods.

THE CYCLOPS

This play by Euripides tells the story of Odysseus and the Cyclops, a one-eyed giant. Arriving at the Cyclops's island, Odysseus and his crew bargain with the giant's captive Silenus. The Cyclops returns and locks them in his cave. Odysseus and his men blind him by driving a stake into his eye, and escape from the cave by hiding under his sheep.

DYSCOLUS

In this comedy by Menander, a rich young man named Sostratus falls in love with a country girl, but fails to impress her grumpy old father Cnemon (the *dyscolus*, or 'bad-tempered man', of the title). The girl's brother Gorgias helps Sostratus, but to no avail. However, after falling down a well, Cnemon has a personality change and hands over control of his affairs to Gorgias, who allows Sostratus to marry his sister. Sostratus's own sister marries Gorgias, and the play ends with a party.

ECCLESIAZUSAE

A political comedy by Aristophanes. By disguising themselves as men, the women, led by Praxagora, take over their city and rule that everyone should have a fair share of love and marriage, including old and ugly people. Praxogara explains this to her husband, who is stuck at home because she has stolen his clothes. Back at the assembly, a young man arrives to find his girlfriend; but he is seized by three old women who fight over him. One wins and carries him away. The play ends with a feast.

ELECTRA

Sophocles and Euripides both wrote tragedies about Electra, daughter of Agamemnon, the king killed by his wife Clytemnestra and her lover Aegisthus (see page 119). In Sophocles' version, Orestes, Agamemnon's son, arrives to avenge the murder. To trick his mother, he sends news that he is dead. Meanwhile, Clytemnestra sends her daughter Chrysothemis to tend Agamemnon's grave. Electra, her other daughter, is furious. They are all arguing at the tomb when they receive the news of Orestes's death. Clytemnestra is delighted, but Electra is devastated and resolves to kill her mother herself. Then Orestes and a friend arrive and kill Clytemnestra and Aegisthus.

Euripides' version is similar, but Electra is married to a farmer. She also helps Orestes to kill their mother.

THE FROGS

This comedy by Aristophanes is one of his most famous. When the play begins, the three great tragic poets, Aeschylus, Sophocles and Euripides, are all dead and the war-weary city of Athens needs good advisers. So the god Dionysus disguises himself as the hero Heracles, and sets off for Hades to fetch Euripides, accompanied by a chorus of frogs.

After many adventures, he is asked to judge a dispute between Aeschylus and Euripides over who is the best poet. Each of them speaks a line of poetry into a pair of scales. Aeschylus wins, as his poetry is the weightiest. However, neither poet has much good advice for Athens.

HIPPOLYTUS

A tragedy by Euripides. When Theseus marries his second wife, Phaedra, she falls in love with his son Hipploytus instead. But the noble Hippolytus refuses to see her, so she hangs herself, leaving a note for Theseus accusing Hippolytus of seducing her. Theseus is furious and banishes his son, calling on the sea god Poseidon to curse him. A monster rises out of the sea and frightens Hippolytus's horses, and he is thrown from his chariot and killed. Theseus finds out too late that Hippolytus was innocent.

MEDEA

One of Euripides's most famous tragedies. The enchantress Medea, wife of the adventurer Jason, has murdered Pelias, one of Jason's enemies. The pair flee to Corinth to escape Pelias's vengeful son. There, Jason decides to leave Medea and marry the daughter of Creon, the King of Corinth. Medea is furious at his ingratitude. King Creon, afraid of her magic, tries to banish her, but she stays long enough to murder Creon and his daughter. Then, to hurt Jason, she kills their own two children, and escapes to Athens.

OEDIPUS TYRANNUS

A tragedy by Sophocles, also called *Oedipus Rex*. Terrified by a prophecy that he will kill his father and marry his mother, Oedipus (or 'swollen-foot', named for his damaged feet) has left his parents, the King and Queen of Corinth. On the road to Thebes he kills a man in a fight, but then wins the hand of the Queen of Thebes, Jocasta, by answering a riddle, so becoming King of Thebes.

But Thebes is troubled by plagues, and an oracle reveals that the killer of Laius, Jocasta's first husband, is in the city. A servant from Corinth arrives to call Oedipus home, as his father has died. Oedipus is afraid of the prophecy, but the servant says Oedipus was not his parent's real son ~ he had been found as a baby. A shepherd reveals that Laius and Jocasta had had a son, but after a prophecy that the son would kill his father, the shepherd had been sent to leave the baby out to die, its feet disabled with a spike. In pity, he had given the baby to a Corinthian instead. Oedipus realizes he was this child. The man he killed was Laius, his father, and his wife is his mother. He goes to find Jocasta, but she has hanged herself. Oedipus blinds himself. Her brother Creon is left to manage the kingdom.

THE ORESTEIA TRILOGY

Many Greek plays were written in groups of four (tetralogies) or three (trilogies). This trilogy of tragedies is by Aeschylus.

Agamemnon Agamemnon returns from the Trojan War with Cassandra, who can see into the future. But his wife Clytemnestra has a new lover, Aegisthus. She also hates Agamemnon for sacrificing their daughter to the gods before the war. She pretends to welcome her husband but then murders him and Cassandra.

Choephoroe Agamemnon's son Orestes, comes with a friend, Pylades, to avenge his father. His sister Electra finds out he has arrived and together they plot against the murderers. Orestes kills first Aegisthus, then Clytemnestra. He sees the Furies, or Eumenides, the spirits of vengeance, coming for him, and runs away.

Eumenides Clytemnestra's ghost urges the Furies to avenge her. Orestes asks the goddess Athene to judge between them, and Athene asks the citizens of Athens to vote on the issue. They are equally divided, and Athene rules that Orestes should be acquitted.

PEACE

A comedy by Aristophanes, set during the war between Athens and Sparta. Trygaios, a vine-grower who is sick of food shortages, rides to heaven on a giant dung-beetle to visit the gods. Hermes explains that most of the gods have gone away to avoid the fighting. War is in charge, and has thrown Peace into a cave. Trygaios and his friends help Peace out of the cave and take her back to Greece. The war ends, and everyone is happy except the weapon-makers.

THE SEVEN AGAINST THEBES

A tragedy by Aeschylus. Oedipus's sons Polyneices and Eteocles are fighting over Thebes. Eteocles holds the city, and Polyneices has a plan for seven champions to lead seven attacks on the city's seven gates. Eteocles picks seven men to defend the gates: he himself will fight his own brother. Both of them die in the battle. It is decreed that Polyneices should not be buried because he attacked his own city. His sister Antigone vows to bury him herself.

THE WASPS

A comedy by Aristophanes. An old man, Philocleon, loves to serve on juries. His son Bdelycleon tries to stop him by keeping him at home, but his friends (dressed as wasps, to show their love of punishing people) try to help him escape. Eventually Bdelycleon lets his father put the family dog on trial for stealing some cheese. After this, the old man changes his ways and goes to a wild party.

BATTLES AND BATTLE FORMATIONS

The Greeks were well-known throughout the ancient world for their superior military skills. Training, discipline and the careful use of battle formations often enabled them to win victories even when they were outnumbered. Here is a list of sites of the most important battles fought by the ancient Greeks, with maps showing what happened at some of the most famous ones.

AEGINA An island between Athens and southern Greece, the site of a naval war between Aegina and Athens in the early 5th century BC.

AEGOSPOTAMI A town near the Hellespont in Turkey. In 405BC, the Athenian navy was virtually wiped out here by the Spartans. It was the last great battle of the Peloponnesian Wars.

CHAERONEA A town in central Greece, the site of Philip II of Macedon's decisive victory over the Greek cities in 338BC.

GAUGAMELA A town on the east side of the Euphrates river, now in Iraq. Here, in 331BC, Alexander the Great won his third victory over King Darius III of Persia.

GRANICUS RIVER A river in northwest Turkey, the scene of Alexander's first victory over the Persians in 334BC.

HYDASPES A river in northwest India and the scene of Alexander's battle against the Indians in 326BC.

ISSUS A river near the borders of present-day Syria and Turkey. It was the site of Alexander's second victory over the Persians in 333BC.

LEUCTRA A town in central Greece, where the Thebans won a victory against the Spartans in 371BC.

MANTINEA A town in southern Greece, where the Thebans won a victory over the Spartans, in 362BC, although they lost the war.

MARATHON A plain in Attica, northeast of Athens. In 490BC, the combined armies of the Athenians and their allies, the Plataeans, won a great victory against the Persians.

This diagram shows the positions of the two armies at the Battle of Marathon.

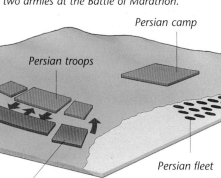

Persian camp

Persian troops

Greek forces begin to encircle the Persians.

Persian fleet

PLATAEA A town in central Greece, the site of a Spartan victory over the Persians in 479BC.

PYDNA The site of the battle in 168BC in which the Romans defeated the Macedonians and took over control of Greece.

RAPHIA A town in Palestine, the scene of a battle in 217BC between the Seleucids and the Ptolemies.

SALAMIS An island just off the coast of Greece, near Athens. In 480BC, the Greeks won a great naval victory here against the Persians during the long-running Persian Wars.

This diagram of the Battle of Salamis shows the positions of the Greek and Persian fleets before the battle began.

Greek fleet

Island of Salamis

Persian fleet

The Greeks are hiding in the bay behind the island, waiting for the Persian fleet to sail up the narrow stretch of water before they attack.

THERMOPYLAE A narrow mountain pass on the east coast of Greece, where the Persians won a great victory in 480BC, during the Persian Wars. King Leonidas of Sparta led his troops in a final brave, but hopeless, battle against the Persians.

This diagram shows the positions of the Spartans and the Persians at the Battle of Thermopylae.

The Spartan troops were trapped.

The Persians approached from two sides at once.

TROY The site of nine cities in Asia Minor, each built on the ruins of its predecessor. The seventh was besieged by the Greeks in about 1250BC, during the Trojan War.

BATTLE FORMATIONS

Greek hoplite soldiers fought in a formation called a phalanx, which consisted of a long block of soldiers (see page 43). For a phalanx to be effective, it was important for the men to stay in line and move as a unit. Flute music was sometimes used to keep them in step with each other and keep the phalanx in line.

A phalanx was usually 8 rows deep, but it could be more or less than that.

Each hoplite was partly protected by his own shield and partly by the shield of the man to his right. This left the man at the right-hand end of the line partly exposed. In a battle, a general would often try to attack the enemy's right wing, as this was the most vulnerable to attack.

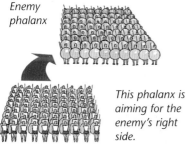

Enemy phalanx

This phalanx is aiming for the enemy's right side.

This is a syntagma, made up of 256 men, the smallest unit of a Macedonian phalanx.

ALEXANDER'S PHALANX

Alexander the Great often used the phalanx in a oblique formation, shown below, as a way of attacking his enemy's weaker right side, while keeping the right side of his own phalanx protected.

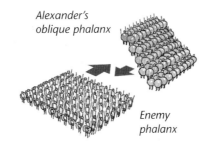

Alexander's oblique phalanx

Enemy phalanx

THE MACEDONIAN PHALANX

The phalanx worked very well, but it was vulnerable if heavy pressure was put on a single point. The Macedonians strengthened the design of the phalanx by using a very long pike, called a sarissa, and a two-handed spear. When the phalanx was charging, the pikes of the first four or five rows of men extended beyond the front line. The rest of the phalanx held their pikes in the air to break the impact of enemy missiles.

The Macedonian syntagma (shown below) had 16 rows, with 16 men in each row.

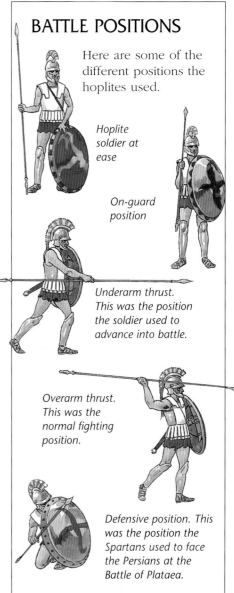

BATTLE POSITIONS

Here are some of the different positions the hoplites used.

Hoplite soldier at ease

On-guard position

Underarm thrust. This was the position the soldier used to advance into battle.

Overarm thrust. This was the normal fighting position.

Defensive position. This was the position the Spartans used to face the Persians at the Battle of Plataea.

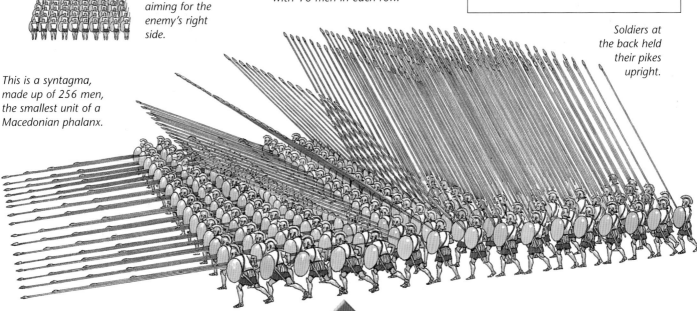

Soldiers at the back held their pikes upright.

WHO'S WHO IN ANCIENT GREECE

The next four pages give you a quick guide to the most famous and most important philosophers, politicians, monarchs, artists, scientists and writers in ancient Greece. Names that appear in **bold type** also have their own entries in the guide.

AESCHYLUS (c.525BC-456BC)

One of the best-known of Greek playwrights, Aeschylus wrote over 80 tragedies, but only seven of them have survived. Most of his plays retold stories about gods, goddesses and Greek heroes. His most famous work is the *Oresteia*, a group of three plays about King Agamemnon and his family (see page 119). The name comes from the central character, Orestes. Aeschylus is known as the founder of Greek tragedy, because he was the first to introduce dialogue and action on stage by using more than one actor at a time. According to legend, he died, aged almost 70, when an eagle dropped a tortoise on his head from a great height.

ALCIBIADES (c.450BC-404BC)

Athenian politician. His father died when he was about four, and he was brought up by **Pericles** and became a pupil of **Socrates**. In 420BC he was elected as a *strategos* (military commander). In the Peloponnesian War, he persuaded the Athenians to send troops to Sicily and was made one of the leaders of the expedition. However, he was accused of having vandalized some statues, and was called back to Athens. Instead he fled to Sparta where he advised the Spartans how to fight their war against Athens. Despite this, the Athenians again elected him as a war commander in 407BC, but he was held responsible for their defeat at the Battle of Notium, and retired. He was assassinated in Persia.

Alexander on his horse Bucephalus

ALEXANDER THE GREAT (356BC-323BC)

Macedonian king and ruthless war general. He was a pupil of **Aristotle**, and learned military tactics as a soldier in the army of his father, **Philip II of Macedonia**. In 336BC Philip was murdered, and Alexander became king at the age of 20. He was a military genius, and in 334BC, after taking control of Greece and the areas to the north, he began an invasion of Asia. Fighting against Darius III of Persia, Alexander conquered so many lands that his empire eventually became the largest in the ancient world.

Alexander was famous for his flamboyant style, and it is said that he always tried to behave like the heroes in the works of the poet **Homer**. In 327 he married a Persian princess named Roxane, and in 331 he founded the city of Alexandria in Egypt. There were many attempts on his life, and he died of a fever in Babylon, aged only 32, after becoming ill at a party ~ perhaps having been poisoned.

ANAXAGORAS (C.500BC-C.428BC)

This early Greek philosopher lived in Athens and was a friend of **Pericles**. In his book, *On Nature*, he tried to explain how the universe worked, and his theories influenced many later philosophers. Anaxagoras calculated that the Sun was a mass of flaming material and that the Moon reflected its light. He was also the first person to explain a solar eclipse.

ANTIGONAS I (c.382BC-301BC)

Macedonian king who tried to gain control of the empire of **Alexander the Great** after Alexander's death in 323BC. Antigonas was killed in the Battle of Ipsus in 301BC, fighting against other leaders who wanted the empire. His descendants, including his son Demetrius I and his grandson Antigonas II, continued to rule over most of Greece until it was eventually conquered by the Romans in 146BC.

ARCHIMEDES (C.287-212BC)

The most famous ancient Greek mathematician, astronomer and inventor. He studied at the Museum (a kind of university) in Alexandria and then lived in Syracuse. He invented a type of pulley for lifting objects, and the Archimedes screw, a device for pumping water.

Archimedes is most famous of all for shouting "Eureka!" (which means "I have found it!") when he discovered an important law of physics while taking a bath. He noticed the water level rising as he climbed in, and realized that the water that he had displaced must have the same volume as his body. This meant that he could measure the volume of unusual-shaped objects and determine their density.

ARISTEIDES (c.520BC-c.467BC)

Athenian politician and general who was known as "the Just" because he was so good, kind and fair. He was a prominent leader at the time of the Persian Wars and was a *strategos* or commander at the Battle of Marathon in 490BC, during the Persian Wars. He later fell out with another politician, **Themistocles**, and was ostracized (banished from Athens) in 482BC. He was called back a year later and took part in the Battles of Salamis and Plataea. Aristeides also helped to set up the Delian League, an alliance of Greek states against the Persians.

ARISTOPHANES (C.445BC-C.385BC)

The most famous Athenian comic playwright. He wrote about 40 comedies, of which eleven survive. They usually make fun of the political events of the time, and some also mock other, more serious playwrights such as **Euripides**. Aristophanes's works won many prizes at the Athens Play Festival. His most famous plays are *The Wasps, The Birds* and *The Frogs*.

ARISTOTLE (384BC-322BC)

The best-known Greek philosopher, Aristotle was son of Nicomachus, doctor to the King of Macedonia. He went to Athens when he was 17 and studied for 20 years at the Academy, the school run by **Plato**. He then went to the eastern Mediterranean, where he researched the lives of animals, and spent three years in Macedonia as the tutor of **Alexander the Great**. He returned to Athens in 335BC and set up his own school, the Lyceum, for the study of science and literature. But after Alexander's death, a new, anti-Macedonian party took power in Athens and Aristotle was forced to leave. He went to Euboea and died there a year later.

Aristotle

Aristotle's writings cover many areas. He invented several sciences, including biology, and the way he divided knowledge up into different subjects, such as psychology and meteorology, still affects science today. His ideas about drama and rhetoric (the power of persuasive speech) are also still influential. Some of Aristotle's most famous works are *Poetics, Politics* and *Metaphysics*.

ASPASIA (born c.465BC)

Aspasia lived with the Athenian leader **Pericles**, and bore him a son. She came from Miletus, and many Athenians did not accept her. She was often mocked by Pericles'

enemies, and by writers of comedies. However she was very beautiful and well-educated, and was admired by **Socrates** and his friends.

CIMON (c.510BC-c.450BC)

Athenian soldier and statesman, renowned for his amazing height and shaggy hair. He was the son of **Miltiades**, and a sworn enemy of the Persians. In 478BC he was made a *strategos* (war commander), and from then on he led many successful campaigns to free the Greek islands from Persian rule. He was most famous for defeating the Persians in a battle at the mouth of the river Eurymedon in about 466BC.

In 462BC, Cimon persuaded Athens to support Sparta, but when the Spartans refused Athenian help, Cimon's prestige suffered and he was ostracized (banished) in 461BC. Later he was called back to Athens to negotiate peace with Sparta. He died during a military expedition to recapture Cyprus from the Persians.

CLEISTHENES (died c.500BC)

Athenian politician. He was a member of the Athenian aristocracy, and took power in Athens after the overthrow of the tyrant Hippias in 510BC. He introduced reforms that led to the political system known as democracy (see page 56), and also introduced ostracism (the practice of banishing unwanted politicians) in Athens. **Pericles** was his nephew.

DRACO (7th century BC)

Athenian politician. In 621BC he was appointed to improve the Athenian legal system and write down all the laws. Draco based his reforms on existing laws, but made them much more severe, and introduced the death penalty for many minor crimes (even laziness was punishable by death!). He also promoted public trials so that people could see that justice had been done. From Draco's harshness, we get the word 'Draconian' which means very severe and strict.

However, the Athenians soon became unhappy with such severe laws, and most of Draco's new system was abolished by **Solon** after he came to power in 594BC.

EUCLID (lived c.300BC)

Little is known about the life of this important Greek mathematician, but we do know that in about 300BC he was working in Alexandria in Egypt. His greatest work was a book called *Elements*, in which he not only explained many aspects of geometry and mathematics, but summed up the teachings of the mathematicians who had lived before him. Several of Euclid's theories and discoveries are still in use today.

EURIPIDES (c.485BC-406BC)

Athenian playwright, and (along with **Aeschylus** and **Sophocles**) one of the three great writers of Greek tragedies. He wrote over 90 plays, of which we know the titles of 80; 19 of them have survived. Among the most famous are *Medea, Bacchae* and *Electra* (see page 122).

Euripides won five first prizes at the Athens Play Festival, and was famous for his natural style and for depicting his characters' inner thoughts and feelings. However, he was criticized for creating evil characters, and was said to be very upset about his unpopularity. In around 408BC he moved to the court of King Archelaus of Macedonia, where he died.

HERODOTUS (c.490BC-c.425BC)

Historian, known as 'the father of history' because he was the first person to establish historical facts and write about them as a sequence of linked events. He was born in Ionia and journeyed around the Mediterranean before moving to Athens. He later settled in Thurii in southern Italy.

His history of the Persian Wars tells us a lot about the Greeks and also about many other ancient peoples (see page 112).

HESIOD (c.700BC)

One of the earliest Greek poets, Hesiod was born on a farm at Ascra in Boeotia. He claimed that the Muses (the nine goddesses of the arts) visited him one day as he was tending sheep on Mount Helicon, and gave him the gift of poetry. His most famous book, *Works and Days*, includes practical details of farming, a calendar of lucky and unlucky days and an explanation of religious ceremonies. He is also thought to have written the *Theogony*, a poetic account of the Greek gods and goddesses and their relationships with each other.

HIPPOCRATES (c.460BC-c.370BC)

Doctor and writer on medicine. His teachings became the basis of medical practice throughout the ancient world (doctors still have to take the Hippocratic Oath, in which they promise to treat their patients well). Unlike many earlier Greek doctors, Hippocrates based his work on close observations of his patients, rather than on religious rituals. His writings (which were collected long after he died, and may not all actually be by him) discuss many aspects of medical practice, including the way a doctor should behave, and the effect of the environment on disease and illness. Hippocrates lived on the island of Kos, where he founded an important medical school.

HOMER (c.8th century BC)

The most famous Greek poet. Little is known about his life. He was a bard ~ an entertainer who recited poems ~ and for centuries his work was passed on by word of mouth. Eventually fragments of it were written down (and probably added to) by other poets and historians, centuries after his death. According to tradition, he came from the island of Chios, and was blind. His poems *The Iliad* and *The Odyssey* describe events during and after the Trojan War (see pages 28-29).

MILTIADES (c.550BC-c.489BC)

Athenian soldier and politician, and father of **Cimon**. In 524BC he was sent to an area called the Chersonese to make sure Athens kept control of the route through to the Black Sea. Later he fought for the Persians, but supported the Ionian revolt against Persian rule in 499BC. When the revolt was crushed he fled to Athens. He led the Athenians at the Battle of Marathon, which the Greeks won. He then led the Athenian fleet in an unsuccessful expedition to Paros, where he was wounded. As a result of this failure he was tried and fined in Athens. He died a short time later.

MYRON (5th century BC)

Athenian sculptor who worked from about 480 to 440BC. His most famous statues included one showing the goddess Athene and the satyr Marsyas, and one called Discobolus, of a man throwing a discus.

PEISISTRATUS (c.600BC-c.527BC)

Athenian politician. In 546BC, after two earlier attempts to seize power, he declared himself tyrant (unelected leader) of Athens. Under his rule, Athens prospered. He reorganized public finances, spent public money on roads and a good water supply, and rebuilt and improved much of Athens. Athenian trade with the rest of Greece also improved. Peisistratus died while still in power and was succeeded by his son Hippias.

PERICLES (c.495BC-429BC)

Athenian statesman who became the most powerful politician of his day. He was elected *strategos* (war commander) every year from 443BC to 429BC, and was a great speaker who could almost always swing public opinion his way. He improved the Athenian democratic system, and built the Parthenon temple; but in 430BC he was charged with stealing public money to fund his building projects, and fined. He was still elected *strategos* the following year, but died in the plague that hit Athens.

PHEIDIAS (c.490BC-c.432BC)

Great Athenian artist who worked as a painter, then a sculptor, and was employed by his friend **Pericles** to provide new sculptures for Athens. Pheidias made the famous bronze statue of Athene which stood on the Acropolis. He was also known for his cult statues in ivory and gold, including a statue of Athene inside the Parthenon, and his masterpiece, a statue of Zeus at Olympia. In 432BC, enemies of Pericles accused Pheidias of stealing the gold given to him for work on the Parthenon. He proved his innocence, but was eventually sent to prison, where he died.

PHILIP II OF MACEDONIA (c.382BC-336BC)

Macedonian king and military leader. He began ruling Macedonia in 359BC. He reorganized the army and showed great skill as a military commander. Within 25 years, Philip had united the country, extended the frontiers, and made

Head of Philip of Macedon

Macedonia the greatest military power of the day. The third of Philip's seven wives was a princess named Olympias: their son, who became **Alexander the Great**, was born in 356BC. Philip was murdered in 336BC and Alexander took over; Olympias and Alexander may have been involved in the plot.

PINDAR (c.518BC-c.438BC)

Poet who was born in Boeotia and journeyed to Athens at an early age. He was a friend of **Aeschylus** and soon became famous for his poetry, which included verses celebrating sporting heroes, and odes to great leaders. Ancient scholars divided his many poems into 17 books, according to their themes and styles. Some later writers described Pindar as the greatest Greek poet of all.

PLATO (427BC-347BC)

Athenian philosopher. He was a member of an aristocratic family and a pupil of **Socrates**. After Socrates was executed, Plato fled to Megara, then lived in Syracuse. Later he returned to Athens, where he wrote *The Apology*, an answer to Socrates' enemies. His ideas for the running of an ideal state were set out in his books *The Republic* and *The Laws*. He founded a school on the outskirts of Athens, which became known as the Academy. The school, whose pupils included **Aristotle**, was famous throughout the ancient world and continued for centuries after Plato's death. It was eventually closed in AD529 by the Roman emperor Justinian, who thought it was politically dangerous. Plato's philosophical ideas have remained influential to the present day.

PRAXITELES (born c.390BC)

Athenian sculptor. Little is known about his life, but some of his original works still exist, including a statue of the god Hermes with the god Dionysus as a baby on his arm. Other sculptures which survive as copies include statues of Aphrodite, Eros and Apollo. Praxiteles developed a new, delicate style of sculpture, leaving behind the grand, formal style of earlier artists.

PYTHAGORAS (c.580BC-c.500BC)

Greek philosopher, mathematician and mystic who was born on the island of Samos, but moved to Croton in Italy where he lived with a large band of devoted followers. He believed in reincarnation and taught his followers that they must not eat meat or beans (no one knows why). He also studied mathematics, astronomy and music, and is most famous for his discoveries about right-angled triangles. Pythagoras never wrote any books, but his teachings and ideas were passed on by his followers and became popular, and many years later they influenced the philosopher **Plato**.

SAPPHO (c.610BC-c.650BC)

A famous poet, Sappho was born on the island of Lesbos, where she spent most of her life (although she spent some of her youth in Sicily). She wrote nine books of poetry, mostly about love or about her family and friends, though only fragments of her work survive. Sappho is famous for her lyrical, emotional style and is regarded as one of the greatest of Greek poets.

SOCRATES (469BC-399BC)

Athenian philosopher. He wrote no books, but taught his pupils by word of mouth, discussing points of philosophy and questioning accepted opinions. Socrates and his followers pointed out weak points in the government and in people's beliefs. He was famous for having a very ugly face but a magnetic personality. However, his teachings made him very unpopular with Athenian politicians. Eventually his enemies charged him with impiety (which meant refusing to believe in the gods) and corrupting the young. He was sentenced to death by poison. His ideas and some of his speeches were written down and passed on by his pupils, who included **Plato**.

SOLON (c.640BC-c.558BC)

Athenian politician. He came to power in about 594BC and quickly introduced a new, more humane system, writing off debts and cancelling many of the harsh laws created by his predecessor **Draco**.

Solon

He set up a new court to which people could appeal if they thought they had been wrongly tried, and reformed the way the government took decisions. Solon also encouraged craftsmen from other parts of Greece to come and live in Athens, and aided the development of trade and industry.

SOPHOCLES (c.496BC-c.405BC)

One of the great tragic playwrights, Sophocles wrote 123 plays. We know the titles of 110, but only seven survive. The most famous are *Electra, Antigone* and *Oedipus Tyrannus*. Sophocles was the first playwright to use more than two actors in his plays, and he was also one of the first to use stage scenery. He was admired for his realistic characters, and he won many prizes at the Athens Play Festival. Sophocles also played a role in Athens society: he was twice elected as a *strategos* (war commander), and was a friend of the historian **Herodotus**.

THEMISTOCLES (c.524BC-c.459BC)

Athenian statesman. He persuaded the Athenians to build up their navy, and was *strategos* (war commander) in the Battle of Salamis in 480BC, which he helped the Greeks to win. However, public opinion turned against him and in c.471BC he was ostracized (banished) and fled to Argos. He was then accused of treason and fled to Asia Minor. The Persians, grateful for his part in negotiating peace with Athens, made him governor of the city of Magnesia.

THUCYDIDES (c.460BC-c.399BC)

Athenian politician and historian. In 424BC, he was elected *strategos*, but he was blamed for a military defeat and fled into exile for over 20 years. While he was away, he wrote an account of the Peloponnesian Wars which is considered to be one of the first history books. As well as describing battles and political events, it reveals a lot about everyday life in Ancient Greece.

XENOPHON (c.428BC-c.354BC)

Athenian writer, and a pupil of **Socrates**. He fought for the Persians and the Spartans against Athens, and was banished to Sparta. There he wrote many books, including *The Anabasis*, about his time with the Persians, and *The Hellenica*, a history of the events of his day.

TIME CHART

This time chart outlines major events in the history of ancient Greece. It also shows - in smaller type, with square bullet points - important things that were happening in other parts of the world at the same time.

This image, taken from a Greek vase painting, is the goddess Europa riding on the back of the god Zeus, depicted as a bull.

EARLY HISTORY

From **40,000BC** The first people settle in Greece, hunting and gathering food.

c.6500-3000BC First inhabitants settle on Crete. Pottery is made in Greece and Crete.

c.5200-2000BC Farming spreads in northern and western Europe.

c.4000BC Evidence of early inhabitants in the Cyclades islands, including remains of metalwork.

c.3400-3300BC The wheel and writing are developed in Sumer in Mesopotamia (now Iraq).

This is what the wheel from a Sumerian chariot might have looked like.

THE BRONZE AGE: C.2900-1000BC

c.2900BC Population of Greece increases, towns develop and metal is widely used.

■ **c.2686-2181BC** Old Kingdom in Egypt. The pyramids are built.

c.2500BC Troy is founded.

■ **c.2500BC** Start of Indus Valley civilization in India. The people build cities and develop writing.
■ **c.2000BC** The building of Stonehenge begins in England.

■ **c.2000BC** Middle Kingdom begins in Egypt.

c.2000BC Possible arrival of the first Greek-speaking people in Greece.

■ **c.1814BC** First Assyrian Empire begins in the Middle East.

c.1900BC Rise of Minoan culture on Crete.

■ **c.1792-1750BC** Reign of Hammurabi, founder of the Babylonian empire.

c.1700BC Cretan palaces are destroyed by earthquakes, then rebuilt.

This golden funeral mask belonged to the Egyptian boy-king, Tutankhamun.

Mycenae in around 1250BC

c.1600BC Rise of Mycenaean culture in Greece.

■ **c.1600BC** Towns and cities develop in China.
■ **c.1567BC** New Kingdom begins in Egypt.
■ **c.1550BC** Aryans settle in northern India and establish the Hindu religion.
■ **c.1500BC** Writing is in use in China.

c.1500-1450BC Traditional date given for the eruption of Thera.

c.1450BC Cretan palaces are destroyed. Knossos is taken over by Mycenaeans and rebuilt. Mycenaean power increases.

c.1400BC Knossos is abandoned.

c.1250BC Main fortifications built at Mycenae and other sites. Traditional date of the start of the Trojan War.

c.1200BC Mycenaean power declines. Migration of Sea Peoples.

- **c.1200BC** Hebrews arrive in Canaan (Palestine) led by Moses and Joshua.
- **c.1200BC** Civilization of the Chavin people begins in Peru, South America.
- **c.1166BC** Death of Ramesses III, one of the greatest Egyptian pharaohs.
- **c.1150BC** Olmec civilization begins in Mexico.

THE DARK AGES: C.1100-800BC

By **1100BC** Mycenaean way of life has collapsed.

- **c.1100BC** Phoenicians spread throughout the Mediterranean and develop alphabetic writing.
- **c.1010-926BC** Kingdom of Israel.
- **c.1000-900BC** Etruscans are established in northern Italy. They are skilled at working in metal.

Bronze sculpture of an Etruscan warrior

- **c.911BC** New Assyrian empire begins.

c.900BC State of Sparta is founded.

Between **850-750BC** Homer probably lived at this time.

- **814BC** Phoenicians found city of Carthage on North African coast.

THE ARCHAIC PERIOD: C.800-500BC

c.800BC Greeks resume trading contacts with other peoples. They adapt Phoenician writing to create an alphabet for their own language.

- **c.800BC** The Hindu religion spreads south in India.

776BC Traditional date of the first Olympic Games, held at Olympia.

- **753BC** Date traditionally given for founding of the city of Rome.

c.750-650BC People start to emigrate from Greece, founding colonies around the Mediterranean and Black Sea.

Vase painting of an Olympic horse race

c.740-720BC Spartans begin expanding their territory, and conquer the nearby state of Messenia.

- **c.700BC** Scythians move into eastern Europe from Asia.

c.650BC Tyrants seize power in Greece. First coins used in Lydia, a kingdom in Asia Minor.

- **c.650BC** Iron Age begins in China.

c.630-613BC Messenians revolt against the Spartans but are defeated.

- **627BC** New Babylonian empire begins.

621BC Draco introduces very strict laws with harsh punishments in Athens.

c.594BC Solon is made archon of Athens and reforms the political system, giving food and rights to the poor.

- **c.550BC** Cyrus II of Persia founds the Persian empire.

c.546BC The Persians conquer Greek colonies in Ionia (Turkey).

- By **521BC** King Darius I has expanded Persian empire from Nile to the Indus.
- **c.510BC** The Roman republic is founded.

508BC Cleisthenes seizes power in Athens and introduces reforms which lead to democracy.

500-494BC Greek colonies in Ionia revolt against Persian rule.

490BC Persians are defeated at the Battle of Marathon.

- **486BC** Death of Siddhartha Gautama, founder of Buddhism.

Carving of the Buddha's head

480BC Persians defeat the Greeks at Thermopylae. Greeks defeat the Persians at the sea-battle of Salamis.

479BC Battle of Plataea: the Persians are defeated and expelled from Greece. Persian fleet is destroyed at Mycale.

A Greek hoplite helmet

445BC 30 Years' Peace declared between Athens and Sparta.

431-404BC The Peloponnesian Wars are fought between the Athenians and their allies (the Delian League) and the Spartans and their allies (the Peloponnesian League).

430BC Athens is hit by plague.

A Greek hoplite soldier

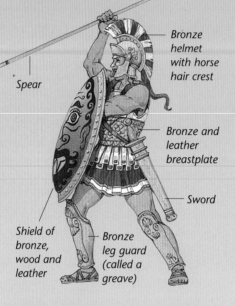

Bronze helmet with horse hair crest

Spear

Bronze and leather breastplate

Sword

Shield of bronze, wood and leather

Bronze leg guard (called a greave)

THE CLASSICAL AGE: c.500-323BC

c.500-336BC The Classical Period in Greek art.

478BC Athens and other Greek states form the Delian League to fight against the Persians.

461-429BC Pericles plays a leading role in Athenian politics. He is elected *strategos* every year from **443BC** until his death in **429BC.**

460-457BC The Long Walls are built around Athens and Piraeus. The Acropolis is rebuilt.

An Athenian black-figure ware pot showing men picking olives.

■ c.450BC Start of the Celtic culture known as La Tène, named after the site in France where evidence of it was first found.

A bronze Celtic shield

449BC The Delian League makes peace with Persia.

421BC 50 Years' Peace negotiated between Sparta and Athens.

420BC Alcibiades is elected *strategos* in Athens.

413BC Athenian fleet goes to Syracuse to intervene in a dispute. The fleet is destroyed and war breaks out again between Athens and Sparta.

407BC Athenian fleet is defeated at Notium.

405BC Athens is defeated by Sparta at sea-battle of Aegospotami.

404BC Final Spartan victory over Athens in the Peloponnesian Wars. The Long Walls are dismantled, the Delian League is dissolved, and Athens is forced to adopt an oligarchic government, known as the Thirty Tyrants.

403BC Democracy restored in Athens.

399BC Wars between Sparta and Persia begin. The philosopher Socrates is condemned to death.

395-387BC Corinthian War: Corinth, Athens, Argos and Thebes fight against Sparta.

394BC Persians defeat the Spartans at the Battle of Cnidus.

394-391BC The Long Walls are rebuilt around Athens.

387BC Corinthian War ends, negotiated by the Persians. Greek colonies in Ionia pass under Persian control.

371BC The Thebans defeat the Spartans at the Battle of Leuctra.

362BC The Spartans and the Athenians defeat the Thebans at the Battle of Mantinea.

359BC Philip II becomes King of Macedonia.

340BC The Greek states form the Hellenic League against threat to Greece posed by Philip of Macedonia.

Macedonian spear head and butt

338BC Philip II defeats the Hellenic League at the Battle of Chaeronea and becomes ruler of Greece. This marks the end of the independence of the Greek city-states.

337BC Greek states join the Corinthian League, led by Philip II. The league declares war on Persia.

336BC Philip II dies, probably murdered, and is succeeded by his son Alexander the Great.

333BC Alexander defeats the Persians at the Battle of Issus.

332BC Alexander conquers Phoenicia, Samaria, Judea, Gaza and Egypt.

331BC Alexander defeats the Persians at Battle of Gaugamela.

327BC Alexander conquers Persia and advances into India.

323BC Alexander dies.

HELLENISTIC AGE: c.323-30BC

323-322BC The Lamian Wars: the city-states fight for independence, but are defeated.

323-281BC The Wars of the Diadochi (Alexander's 'successors').

- ■ **c.300BC** The end of the Chavin civilization in South America.
- ■ **c.300BC** Mayan people begin building stone cities in Central America.

The lighthouse at Alexandria in Egypt was one of the great achievements of the Hellenistic Age.

Greek soldiers shown on a vase painting

301BC Battle of Ipsus: four rival Diadochi kingdoms are established.

281BC Three Diadochi kingdoms are set up: Macedonia (ruled by Antigonas); Asia Minor (ruled by Seleucus); and Egypt (ruled by Ptolemy).

275BC King Pyrrhus of Epirus is defeated by the Romans in Italy.

266-262BC Chremonides War: the Athenians' rebellion is defeated.

■ **221-206BC** Ch'in dynasty in China.

215BC Philip V of Macedonia allies with Hannibal of Carthage in the Punic Wars between the Carthaginians and the Romans, provoking Roman reprisals.

This gold ornament may have been made for a Chavin priest.

215-205BC First Macedonian War between Macedonians and Romans.

■ **214BC** Great Wall built in China.

202BC Philip V of Macedonia forms an alliance with the Seleucid empire.

202-197BC The Second Macedonian War. Philip V is defeated by the Romans and surrenders control of Greece.

179-168BC Reign of the last Macedonian king, Perseus.

171-168BC Third Macedonian War: the Romans defeat Perseus at the Battle of Pydna and set up four Roman republics.

147-146BC The Achaean War: the Romans destroy Corinth after a Macedonian revolt, and impose direct Roman rule on Greece.

64BC The Seleucid empire comes under the rule of the Roman empire.

31BC Battle of Actium: Octavian defeats Mark Antony and Cleopatra VII, Queen of Egypt (a Ptolemy), in a sea battle.

30BC Egypt becomes a province of the Roman empire.

This is a portrait of Octavian, who became Rome's first emperor, taking the name Augustus.

GLOSSARY

This glossary explains many specialized and Greek words used in this book that may be unfamiliar. There are also definitions of other words connected with ancient Greece, that you may come across. If a word in the text of an entry has its own separate entry, it is shown in *italics*.

acropolis Meaning 'high city', it was a fortified city, built on high ground. In *Mycenaean* times, the royal palace was on the acropolis, but from the *Archaic Period*, the acropolis was kept for temples.

agora An open space, in the middle of a Greek city, used for markets and as a meeting place.

Amphidromia A ceremony held after the birth of a baby, usually involving the naming of the baby.

amphora (plural: *amphorae*) A large pot with two handles used for wine and other liquids.

andron A dining room in a private house, used only by the men.

Anthesteria A spring festival, in which three-year-old children were presented with a jug, as a symbol that they were no longer infants.

Archaic Period The period in Greek history from about 800-500BC, after the *Dark Ages* and before the *Classical Period*.

architrave The lowest part of the *entablature* on a temple.

archon An Athenian official. Very powerful in the *Archaic Period*, but in the *Classical Period* the role of an archon was mainly ceremonial.

aristocrat A member of a rich, land-owning family. Aristocrats ruled the city-states in the *Archaic Period*. The name comes from the Greek *aristoi*, meaning 'the best people'.

Asia Minor The historical name for Anatolia, the Asian part of Turkey, between the Black Sea, the Aegean and the Mediterranean.

Asphodel Fields In Greek mythology, a drab, misty place where most people, who had been neither very good nor very bad, were sent after they died.

Attica The state of Athens and the surrounding countryside.

barbarian The name for any foreigner who did not speak Greek. The word came from the strange "bar-bar-bar" noise that the Greeks thought foreigners made.

black-figure ware A style of pottery decorated with black figures on a red background.

Bronze Age The period from c.3000-1100BC during which bronze was the most important metal, used for making tools and weapons.

capital The top part of a column.

caryatid A statue of a young woman used in place of a column.

cella The main room of a temple, containing the *cult statue* of the god or goddess.

centaur A creature from Greek mythology, with the head, arms and upper body of a man and the lower body and legs of a horse.

Chaos The state of nothingness before the world began.

chiton A woman's dress, made from one or two pieces of cloth, fastened at the shoulders.

chorus A group of men who took part in plays. They all spoke together, often commenting on the action, and sang and danced too.

citizen A free man who had the right to participate in the government of the city-state in which he was born.

Classical Period The period in Greek history from about 500-338BC, between the end of the Persian Wars and the conquest of Greece by Philip II of Macedonia.

Corinthian column An ornate style of column, popular with the Ancient Romans, with a capital decorated with a leafy pattern.

cornice The ledge on a temple above the *pediment*.

cuirass A breastplate and backplate used by Greek *hoplite* soldiers. It was made of bronze or leather and bronze, and joined together by leather straps.

cult statue A statue in the main room of a temple of the god or goddess to which the temple was dedicated. People addressed their prayers to the cult statue.

Dark Ages The period in Greek history about which relatively little is known. This dates roughly from the decline of the *Mycenaeans*, after about 1100BC, to the first signs of a revival in about 800BC.

Delian League An alliance formed by Athens and its allies, in 478-477BC, to fight the Persians. Still in existence, though smaller, during the Peloponnesian Wars.

democracy A political system, introduced by the ancient Greeks, in which all citizens had a say in the running of their state. The word comes from the Greek words *demos*, meaning 'people', and *kratos*, meaning 'rule'.

Diadochi The name given to the generals who took over different parts of Alexander the Great's empire after his death.

Dionysia A dramatic festival, held by the Athenians, from which the idea of plays probably developed.

Dorians A people who became dominant in southern Greece in around 1100BC, after the decline of the *Mycenaean* civilization. Their dialect formed the basis for the Classical Greek language.

Doric column A style of column with a plain, undecorated capital. The distinguishing feature of a style of architecture known as the Doric Order.

electrum A naturally occuring mixture of gold and silver, which was used to make the first coins.

Elysian Fields The equivalent of Heaven in Greek mythology.

entablature The part of a temple above the columns and below the *pediment*.

ephebe A young Athenian man on two years' military training.

ephor A Spartan official. Five ephors were elected every year to oversee the running of the state.

Etruscans A people who established a civilization in northern Italy between about 800BC and 400BC.

faience A type of glazed material, often used by the *Minoans* to make decorative objects.

fresco A wall painting made by applying paint to wet plaster.

frieze Horizontal band between the *cornice* and the *entablature* on a Greek temple, usually decorated with sculpture.

gerousia A Spartan council, consisting of two kings and 28 council members, elected for life.

gorgon From Greek mythology, one of three winged monstrous sisters, with snakes for hair and huge teeth. Anyone who looked at them was turned into stone.

grammatistes A teacher of reading, writing and arithmetic.

greave A bronze covering used by Greek *hoplite* soldiers to protect the leg from knee to ankle.

gymnasium (plural: *gymnasia*) A sports hall for athletic training. Later, it was often a place of intellectual activity too, equipped with a lecture hall and a library.

gynaeceum The women's rooms in a private house.

Hellene The word the Greeks used to refer to the whole Greek race. From the name of a legendary hero, Hellen, who was said to be the father of the race.

Hellenistic Age A term used to describe the period after the death of Alexander the Great in 323BC, and before the conquest of Egypt by the Romans in 30BC, when Greek language and culture dominated the countries of Alexander's former empire.

Hellenistic World The area of the Mediterranean and the Middle East - including Italy, Turkey, Egypt, Syria and Lebanon - that was influenced by Greek civilization and culture. This was roughly equivalent to the extent of Alexander's former empire.

helot Descendants of the people who had resisted Spartan rule, who were made to work as slaves.

herm A statue of the god Hermes, consisting of a head on a pillar. It usually stood outside the front door of a house and was thought to protect the home.

hetaira (plural: *hetairai*) A woman educated to make witty conversation, play music and sing, to entertain men at dinner.

hieroglyphics Any writing system based on picture symbols.

himation A cloak or shawl, worn by both men and women.

Hittites A people who built an empire in *Asia Minor* between about 2000BC and 1200BC

hoplite A heavily armed foot soldier, who fought in the armies of the Greek city-states.

Immortal Another word for a god or goddess. Some Greek heroes became Immortals.

Ionic column A slender column, with a capital decorated with a curling pattern, called a volute. The main feature of a style of architecture called the Ionic Order.

kitharistes A teacher of music and poetry.

kore A sculpture of a young woman from the *Archaic Period*.

kouros A sculpture of a young man from the *Archaic Period*.

krater A large vase in which wine was mixed with water.

labrys A double-headed weapon, which was an important sacred symbol in *Minoan* religion.

labyrinth A mythical underground maze at Knossos on Crete, and home of a bull-headed monster called the *Minotaur*.

libation A liquid offering to the gods, of wine, milk or blood. It was usually poured over an altar or onto the earth during a religious ceremony.

Linear A An early form of writing used by the *Minoans*.

Linear B A form of writing used by the *Mycenaeans*, adapted from *Linear A*.

Long Walls Walls which enclosed the city of Athens and its port at Piraeus from 460-404BC. Demolished by the Spartans at the end of the Peloponnesian Wars.

lost wax casting A method of casting bronze statues, first using a wax model around a clay core.

lyre A stringed musical instrument, made from a tortoise shell and the horns of an ox.

megaron A large hall in a *Mycenaean* palace, where the king conducted state business. It usually contained four pillars and a hearth.

metic A free man living in Athens, but born outside the city. A metic had to pay taxes and serve in the army, but could never become a *citizen* or own property.

Minoan The name given by archaeologist Arthur Evans to the civilization he discovered on Crete. The term came from the legendary Cretan king, Minos.

Minotaur The legendary bull-headed monster who lived in the *labyrinth* at Knossos on Crete.

mosaic A design or picture made up of small pieces of glass or stone. Used by the Ancient Greeks to decorate floors.

Museum The Latin name for a temple to the Muses, goddesses of the arts and creativity, from the Greek word *Museion*. The most famous museum was built in Alexandria, in Egypt. It became a great institution of learning, and a base for scientists and inventors.

Mycenaean A civilization on mainland Greece, dating back to around 1900BC, named after the city of Mycenae, where evidence of the culture was first discovered.

mystery cult A religious cult, with secret rituals and ceremonies, open only to those who had passed certain tests.

oligarchy A political system involving rule by a small group. It means 'rule by the few' in Greek.

omen A sign from the gods, which warned of good or evil to come. Specially trained priests interpreted omens from marks on the livers of sacrificed animals, or from the flight patterns of birds.

oracle One of three things: a message given by a god or goddess, the priest or priestess who spoke on their behalf, or the sacred place where this happened. The most famous oracle was at Delphi, where a priestess called the *Pythia* was thought to communicate with the god Apollo.

orientalizing style A style of Greek pottery in use from around 720-550BC. Pots were decorated with motifs such as lotuses, palms and mythical beasts, which were popular in Middle Eastern art.

ostracism A vote held in the Athenian Assembly to banish unpopular politicians. The word comes from the pieces of broken pottery, called *ostraka*, on which the voters wrote names of the people they wanted to expel.

paidagogos A special slave who escorted a boy to and from school and supervised him in class.

paidotribes A teacher of dancing and athletics.

pankration A dangerous sport, combining wrestling and boxing.

patron deity A god or goddess who was thought to protect a particular place, person or group of people. For example, Athene was the patron goddess of Athens.

pediment The triangular part at the front and back of a temple, above the *entablature* and below the *cornice*. It was often decorated with painted sculptures.

Peloponnesian League An alliance formed by Sparta and its allies to fight Athens and its allies in the Peloponnesian Wars.

peltast A lightly armed foot soldier, used by the Greek armies.

pentathlon An event at the Olympic Games made up of running, jumping, wrestling and discus and javelin-throwing. From the Greek *pente*, meaning 'five', and *athlon*, meaning 'contest'.

periokoi Descendants of the people who had surrendered to Spartan rule.

peristyle A row of columns, or colonnade, that surrounds the outside of a temple.

phalanx A battle formation used by *hoplite* soldiers in ancient Greek armies.

philosopher From the Greek for 'lover of knowledge', the first philosophers were scholars who studied all aspects of the world around them, including the purpose of the universe and the nature of human life.

Phoenicians A people from the eastern Mediterranean, who lived on the coast of what is now Lebanon. They were great traders and explorers and they devised an alphabet which formed the basis for the Classical Greek one.

pithos (plural: *pithoi*) A large, pottery storage jar used in Crete.

polis An independent Greek state, consisting of a city and the surrounding countryside.

psiloi Auxiliary soldiers, armed with clubs and stones.

Pythia The priestess who spoke on behalf of the god Apollo at the Oracle of Delphi.

red-figure ware A style of pottery, with red figures painted on a black background.

relief A sculpture carved on panels of stone. The stone was cut away so that a scene stood out against a flat background.

rhapsode A man who made his living by reciting poetry at religious festivals or private parties.

rhyton A special pot, in the shape of a horn or an animal's head. It was used in religious ceremonies to make a *libation*.

sacrifice An offering of food made to a god or goddess. An animal sacrifice involved killing the animal.

sarcophagus A stone coffin.

Sea Peoples The name given to a group of people who migrated around the eastern Mediterranean in around 1190BC. It is thought that they my have come from Greece, its islands and colonies.

shaft grave An early *Mycenaean* tomb, in which the body was buried at the bottom of a hole up to 12m (40 feet) deep.

soothsayer Someone who was thought to be able to predict the future. A famous example was the Trojan princess Cassandra, who warned the people of Troy that the Trojan horse was a trick.

sophist A teacher of public speaking and debating skills, who went from city to city.

stele (plural:*stelae*) A stone slab used to mark a grave.

stoa (plural:*stoae*) A long, roofed passageway with columns, which provided shelter from the sun and rain. It usually surrounded a marketplace, or *agora*, in the middle of a Greek town, and it sometimes contained stores or offices.

strategos (plural: *strategoi*) An Athenian army commander and political leader. There were ten *strategoi,* elected annually, and they were in charge of implementing policies decided by the Council and Assembly.

Styx In Greek mythology, the river a dead person had to be ferried across in order to reach the afterlife.

symposium A dinner party for men, which included drinking, intellectual conversation and music.

Tartarus The ancient Greek equivalent of Hell.

terracotta A mixture of unfired clay, sand, and particles of clay that have already been baked. It was used to make tiles and small statues, which are sometimes known as terracottas.

Thirty Tyrants The group of pro-Spartan aristocrats, led by a man called Critias, who ruled Athens after its defeat in the Peloponnesian Wars. They proved so unpopular that the Spartans eventually allowed *democracy* to be restored.

tholos A *Mycenaean* grave consisting of a beehive-shaped room entered through a long corridor. Later, the name was also given to circular buildings with conical roofs, often with pillars around the outside.

Titan One of a family of giants, children of Gaea, mother Earth, and Uranus, the sky, who were the first gods and goddesses in Greek mythology.

trireme A powerful ancient Greek warship with three rows of oarsmen.

tyrant From the Greek word for "ruler", someone who governed with absolute power, often one who had overthrown the previous ruler. In the *Archaic Period,* many Greek states were governed by tyrants. Later, a tyrant meant any cruel, oppressive ruler.

Underworld The kingdom of the Dead, deep under the Earth's surface. Also known as Hades.

INDEX

BC, AD AND c.

Many of the dates in this book have the letters **BC**, **AD** or **c.** next to them.

- **BC** stands for "Before Christ". BC dates are counted backwards from the birth of Christ ~ so 300BC means 300 years before the birth of Christ.

- **AD** is used with dates after the birth of Christ, such as 50AD. It stands for *Anno Domini*, which is Latin for "Year of the Lord". It is often used for dates from Greek and Roman times.

- Some dates have a **c.** in front of them. It stands for *circa* ~ the Latin word for "about". It means that the date is not exact, but only a rough guess. It is used when experts are not sure exactly when something happened.

ACKNOWLEDGEMENTS

Every effort has been made to trace the copyright holders of the material in this book. If any rights have been omitted, the publishers offer to rectify this in any subsequent editions following notification. The publishers are grateful to the following organizations and individuals for their permission to reproduce the material on the following pages (t=top, b=bottom, l=left, r=right, c=central):

- **AKG London: p81** tr; **p83** t and **p84** l © Erich Lessing.
- **Ancient Art & Architecture Collection:** p21 c; p21 tr; p26 r; p27 tl; p27 bl; p32; p38 l; p53 tr; p55 l; pp86-87; p95 b.
- **British Museum: p37** b Cat. E86 Vases; **p62** tr Cat. 2818 Bronze; **p62** l Cat. E135 Vases; **p62** b Cat. 869 Sculpture; **p64** t Cat. E219 Vases; **pp66-67** Cat. 1920.12-21.1 Vases; **p67** tl Cat. D13 Vases; **p82** Cat. 1873.8-20.385; **p88** l, Cat. F267 Vases; **pp88-89** Cat. E68 Vases; **p91** t Cat. D16 A Sculpture; **p94** Cat. 266; **p102** Cat. 1930.4-17.1; **pp108-109**, Cat. 2113.
- **C. M. Dixon: p11; p15** br; **p17** br; **p18** tr; **p19** t; **p21** cl; **p23** b; **p25** tr; **p30** l; **p39** b; **p44** t; **p47** r; **p50** tr; **p50** br; **p56** tr; **p58** t; **p66** tl; **p67** c; **p68** r; **p80** br; **pp84-85 ; p88** r; **p93** t; **pp94-95; p95** t; **p95** r; **p97** tr; **p98** b; **p99** tr.
- **Corbis: Title page (pp2-3)** /Michael Nicholson; **Contents page (pp4-5)** /Wolfgang Kaehler; **p6** bl /Mimmo Jodice; **p8** t /David Lees; **pp8-9** /Jonathan Blair; **p9** tr /Araldo de Luca; **p9** cr /Yann Arthus-Bertrand; **p9** br /Araldo de Luca; **pp12-13** /Anthony Bloomfield, Cordai Photo Library; **p13** r /Seattle Art Museum; **p28** bl /Araldo de Luca; **p33** /Gianni Dagli Orti; **p34** t /Archivo Iconografico, S.A; **pp34-35** /Adam Woolfitt; **p35** t /Gianni Dagli Orti; **p35** r /Michael Boys; **p51** /Scheufler Collection; **p56** b /Bettman; **p58** c /Fulvio Roiter; **p59** b /Paul A. Souders; **p63** /Gianni Dagli Orti; **p76** /Andrea Jemolo; **p77** c /Vanni Archive; **p77** br /Richard T. Nowitz; **p78** t /Corbis; **p78** c /Gianni Dagli Orti; **p78** bl /Gianni Dagli Orti; **p80** l /Gianni Dagli Orti; **p80** c /David Lees; **p80** cr /Gianni Dagli Orti; **p81** tl /Araldo de Luca; **p88** r /Michael T. Sedam; **p93** c /Araldo de Luca; **p96** /Gianni Dagli Orti; **p97** r /Arte & Immagini srl; **p99** b /Wolfgang Kaehler; **pp100-101** /Archivo Iconografico S. A.; **p101** tr /Chris Hellier; **p103** /Paul Almasy; **p104** /Gianni Dagli Orti; **p105** br /Gianni Dagli Orti; **p106** t /Araldo de Luca; **pp106-107** /John Noble; **p107** t /Gianni Dagli Orti; **p108** bl /Angelo Hornak; **p108** c /Archivo Iconografico S. A.; **p109** /Roger Wood; **p112** tr /Archivo Iconografico S. A.; **p112** bl /Archivo Iconografico S. A.; **p115** /Gianni Dagli Orti; **Endpapers** /Kevin Schaffer.
- **Deutsches Archäologisches Institut, Athens:** p64 bl.
- **Digital Vision:** p6 background; p20; p121 © Digital Vision.
- **ET Archive:** p16 br; p29 tr; p43 br /British Museum; p81 br /Musée du Louvre, Paris; p83 b /Archaeological Museum, Ferrara.
- **Hunterian Museum, Glasgow University:** p75.
- **Katz Pictures:** p21 b; pp38-39 / The Mansell Collection.
- **National Archaeological Museum, Athens:** p54 tr.
- **Numismatic Museum, Athens:** p61 tr.
- **Photostage:** p91 b © Donald Cooper.
- **Popperfoto:** p110 br /Reuters.
- **Scala:** p22 b /National Museum, Athens; p65 tr /Archaeological Museum, Istanbul; p98 t /Acropolis Museum, Athens.
- **Staatliche Museum, Berlin:** p65 bl /Bildarchiv Preussischer Kulturbesitz/Johannes Laurentius.
- **Staatliche Museum, Munich:** p70 r /Staatliche Antikensammlungen und Glyptothek München.
- **Tony Stone:** pp72-73 © Steve Outram.
- **Trireme Trust:** p44 b © Paul Lipke.
- **Werner Forman Archive:** p55 r.

Every effort has been made to trace the copyright holders of the material in this book. If any rights have been omitted, the publishers offer to rectify this in any subsequent editions following notification. The publishers are grateful to the organizations and individuals who have given their permission to reproduce the material.

First published in 2007 by Usborne Publishing Ltd, Usborne House, 83-85 Saffron Hill, London EC1N 8RT, England.
www.usborne.com Copyright © 2007, 2002 Usborne Publishing Ltd.